D1489442

COUNTRY CROCHET

McCall's Needlework & Crafts

COUNTRY CROCHET

McCall's Needlework & Crafts

MEREDITH® PRESS
New York, New York

DEAR CROCHETER:

Meredith Press is pleased to offer you this sampling of delightful
crochet projects created by *McCall's Needlework & Crafts*
magazine. In this country collection, the designers bring a sense
of fun and familiarity to home furnishings and accessories.

Amidst this selection of traditional crochet projects such as
afghans and tablecloths, you'll find more than a few surprises,
including a handworked chess set, a delicate welcome wreath,
and a plush assembly of barnyard animals.

We at Meredith have considered your interests—from practical
to whimsical—and have enjoyed bringing them to you in this
special book. Accompanying the 16 projects are clear, easy-to-
follow directions and large, full-color photographs. We hope all
this adds up to a favorable addition to your craft library.

Sincerely,

Connie Schrader

The Editors

Meredith ® Press is an imprint of Meredith ® Books:

President, Book Group: Joseph J. Ward
Vice President. Editorial Director: Elizabeth P. Rice

For Meredith Press:

Executive Editor: Connie Schrader
Project Manager: Barbara Machtiger
Project Editor: Gloria Mosesson
Editorial Assistants: Valerie Martone and Carolyn Mitchell
Production Manager: Bill Rose

ISBN: 0-696-02354-7 (hard cover)
ISBN: 0-696-02374-1 (trade paperback)
Library of Congress Card Number: 90-063669

Packaged by Rapid Transcript, a division of March Tenth, Inc.
Design by Stanley S. Drate/Folio Graphics Co., Inc.

Printed in the United States of America
10 9 8 7 6 5 4 3 2 1

CONTENTS

INTRODUCTION

Crochet is an old and highly flexible needle art. Just think of all the ways that crocheted fabrics can be shaped and molded while other handicrafts cannot. Crochet lends itself to an enormous range of materials, from the finest thread suitable for lacemaking to coarse, heavy twine, with hook sizes to accommodate all. And the finished products can be bent, stretched, blocked, and altered with amazing ease and variety.

Think, too, of the speed with which crochet is practiced. One hardly ever sees a crochet hook moving slowly. It's satisfying to complete projects relatively rapidly, especially for a beginner or a child, and there are so many easy projects to start with that novices quickly fall in love with their newfound skills. It is, perhaps, the easiest craft to which a young person can be introduced.

Crochet also adjusts to the creation of small objects and to limited amounts of raw materials. So it is an economical art that lets you use up odds and ends of yarns and threads and a host of other materials.

The pages that follow offer an interesting variety of crocheted items for every room in the house and for every member of the family. Projects both delicate and practical are featured for the bedroom and bath, including a filet crochet bedspread, pillows, and table drape. The bath gets a country lift with crocheted edgings and trims on towels, a pocketed catchall, and a unique panel insert for the medicine cabinet. Accessories for the kitchen and dining area abound in such welcoming touches as a breakfast ensemble that features place mats, napkin rings, a hot pad, and a napkin holder that can be stenciled to coordinate with your dishes. There are charming appliance "cozies" as well as a beautiful Lacy Medallion Table Cover to use for more formal occasions.

The chapter entitled "Decorative Show-Offs" features handsome projects for display: a group of country boxes in various shapes, a choice of welcoming wreaths for wall or door, and a selection of items to crochet in popular quilt motifs.

For the younger set, what could be cuter than a group of crocheted figures representing Old MacDonald and his farmyard friends? And, to coordinate a child's room, try the crocheted black-and-red scottie motif projects that feature a pillow toy, a loop-stitch rug, a wall hanging with storage pockets, and an afghan.

You're sure to enjoy selecting from among the many projects for everyday use and special occasions that have been chosen for their appealing country look.

CROCHET FOR BEDROOM AND BATH

Personalize your boudoir with the versatility of crochet. Boudoir includes both bedroom and bath. Crochet lends itself to both the delicate and the practical, as you'll see in the items that follow.

Delicate Country Charm

Here is a pretty, lacy ensemble for a special bedroom. Filet squares are joined to create the bedspread, ruffled pillow shams, and table drape.

FILET SQUARE BEDSPREAD

SIZE: 72″ × 86″
MATERIALS: DMC Cébélia Fil d'Ecosse, size 10, forty-five 282-yard balls white. Steel crochet hook No. 8 (1.25 mm) or size required to obtain gauge.
GAUGE: 21 tr = 2″; 3 rows = 1″. Each motif is 14″ square.
BEDSPREAD: FIRST SQUARE: Beg at center of square, ch 6. Sl st in first ch to form ring.

Rnd 1: Ch 4 (counts as first tr), 4 tr in ring, (ch 5, 5 tr in ring) 3 times; ch 5, sl st in top of ch-4.
Rnd 2: Ch 4, tr in 4 tr, (4 tr, ch 7, 4 tr in corner sp, tr in 5 tr) 3 times, 4 tr, ch 7, 4 tr in last sp, sl st in top of ch-4.
Rnd 3: Ch 7, sk 3 tr, tr in next tr, ch 3, sk 3 tr, tr in next tr, * ch 3, tr, ch 7, tr in 4th ch of corner sp, ch 3, tr in next tr, (ch 3, sk 3 tr, tr in next tr) 3 times, repeat from * twice, ch 3, tr, ch 7, tr in 4th ch of corner sp, ch 3, tr in next tr, ch 3, sl st in 4th ch of ch-7.
Rnd 4: Ch 7, tr in next tr, ch 3, tr in next tr, 3 tr in

next sp, tr in next tr, * 4 tr, ch 7, 4 tr in corner sp, tr in next tr, 3 tr in next sp, tr in next tr, (ch 3, tr in next tr) 3 times, 3 tr in next sp, tr in next tr, repeat from * twice, 4 tr, ch 7, 4 tr in corner sp, tr in next tr, 3 tr in next sp, tr in next tr, ch 3, sl st in 4th ch of ch-7.

Rnd 5: Ch 7, tr in next tr, 3 tr in next sp, tr in 9 tr, * 4 tr, ch 7, 4 tr in corner sp, tr in 9 tr, 3 tr in next sp, tr in next tr, ch 3, tr in next tr, 3 tr in next sp, tr in 9 tr, repeat from * twice, 4 tr, ch 7, 4 tr in corner sp, tr in 9 tr, 3 tr in next sp, sl st in 4th ch of ch-7.

Rnd 6: Ch 7, tr in next tr, (ch 3, sk 3 tr, tr in next tr) 4 times, * ch 3, tr, ch 7, tr in 4th ch of corner sp, ch 3, tr in next tr, (ch 3, sk 3 tr, tr in next tr) 4 times, ch 3, tr in next tr, (ch 3, sk 3 tr, tr in next tr) 4 times, repeat from * twice, ch 3, tr, ch 7, tr in 4th ch of corner sp, ch 3, tr in next tr, (ch 3, sk 3 tr, tr in next tr) 3 times, ch 3, sl st in 4th ch of ch-7.

Rnd 7: Ch 7, tr in next tr, (ch 3, tr in next tr) 3 times, (3 tr in next sp, tr in next tr) twice, * 4 tr, ch 7, 4 tr in corner sp, tr in next tr, (3 tr in next sp, tr in next tr) twice, (ch 3, tr in next tr) 7 times, (3 tr in next sp, tr in next tr) twice, repeat from * twice, 4 tr, ch 7, 4 tr in corner sp, tr in next tr, (3 tr in next sp, tr in next tr) twice, (ch 3, tr in next tr) twice, ch 3, sl st in 4th ch of ch-7.

Rnd 8: Ch 7, tr in next tr, (ch 3, tr in next tr) twice, 3 tr in next sp, tr in each of next 13 tr, * 4 tr, ch 7, 4 tr in corner sp, tr in each of next 13 tr, 3 tr in next sp, tr in next tr, (ch 3, tr in next tr) 5 times, 3 tr in next sp, tr in each of next 13 tr, repeat from * twice, 4 tr, ch 7, 4 tr in corner sp, tr in each of next 13 tr, 3 tr in next sp, tr in next tr, ch 3, tr in next tr, ch 3, sl st in 4th ch of ch-7.

Rnd 9: Ch 7, tr in next tr, (ch 3, tr in next tr) twice, (ch 3, sk 3 tr, tr in next tr) 5 times, * ch 3, tr, ch 7, tr in 4th ch of corner sp, ch 3, tr in next tr, (ch 3, sk 3 tr, tr in next tr) 5 times, (ch 3, tr in next tr) 5 times, (ch 3, sk 3 tr, tr in next tr) 5 times, repeat from * twice, ch 3, tr, ch 7, tr in 4th ch of corner sp, ch 3, tr in next tr, (ch 3, sk 3 tr, tr in next tr) 5 times, ch 3, tr in next tr, ch 3, sl st in 4th ch of ch-7.

Rnd 10: Ch 7, tr in next tr, (ch 3, tr in next tr) 5 times, (3 tr in next sp, tr in next tr) 3 times, * 4 tr, ch 7, 4 tr in corner sp, tr in next tr, (3 tr in next sp, tr in next tr) 3 times, (ch 3, tr in next tr) 11 times, (3 tr in next sp, tr in next tr) 3 times, repeat from * twice, 4 tr, ch 7, 4 tr in 4th ch of corner sp, tr in next tr, (3 tr in next sp, tr in next tr) 3 times, (ch 3, tr in next tr) 4 times, ch 3, sl st in 4th ch of ch-7.

Rnd 11: Ch 7, tr in next tr, (ch 3, tr in next tr) 4 times, 3 tr in next sp, tr in each of 17 tr, * 4 tr, ch 7, 4 tr in corner sp, tr in each of 17 tr, 3 tr in next sp, tr in next tr, (ch 3, tr in next tr) 9 times, 3 tr in next sp, tr in each of 17 tr, repeat from * twice, 4 tr, ch 7, 4 tr in corner sp, tr in each of 17 tr, 3 tr in next sp, tr in next tr, (ch 3, tr in next tr) 3 times, ch 3, sl st in 4th ch of ch-7.

Rnd 12: Ch 7, tr in next tr, (ch 3, tr in next tr) 4 times, (ch 3, sk 3 tr, tr in next tr) 6 times, ch 3, * tr, ch 7, tr in 4th ch of corner sp, ch 3, tr in next tr, (ch 3, sk 3 tr, tr in next tr) 6 times, (ch 3, tr in next tr) 9 times, (ch 3, sk 3 tr, tr in next tr) 6 times, ch 3, repeat from * twice, tr, ch 7, tr in 4th ch of corner sp, ch 3, tr in next tr, (ch 3, sk 3 tr, tr in next tr) 6 times, (ch 3, tr in next tr) 3 times, ch 3, sl st in 4th ch of ch-7.

Rnd 13: Ch 4, 3 tr in next sp, tr in next tr, (ch 3, tr in next tr) 7 times, (3 tr in next sp, tr in next tr) 4 times, * 4 tr, ch 7, 4 tr in corner sp, tr in next tr, (3 tr in next sp, tr in next tr) 4 times, (ch 3, tr in next tr) 7 times, 3 tr in next sp, tr in next tr, (ch 3, tr in next tr) 7 times, (3 tr in next sp, tr in next tr) 4 times, repeat from * twice, 4 tr, ch 7, 4 tr in corner sp, tr in next tr, (3 tr in next sp, tr in next tr) 4 times, (ch 3, tr in next tr) 6 times, ch 3, sl st in top of ch-4.

Rnd 14: Ch 7, sk 3 tr, tr in next tr, 3 tr in next sp, tr in next tr, (ch 3, tr in next tr) 5 times, 3 tr in next sp, tr in each of 21 tr, * 4 tr, ch 7, 4 tr in corner sp, tr in each of 21 tr, 3 tr in next sp, tr in next tr, (ch 3, tr in next tr) 5 times, 3 tr in next sp, tr in next tr, ch 3, sk 3 tr, tr in next tr, 3 tr in next sp, tr in next tr, (ch 3, tr in next tr) 5 times, 3 tr in next sp, tr in each of 21 tr, repeat from * twice, 4 tr, ch 7, 4 tr in corner sp, tr in each of 21 tr, 3 tr in next sp, tr in next tr, (ch 3, tr in next tr) 5 times, 3 tr in next sp, sl st in 4th ch of ch-7.

Rnd 15: Ch 4, 3 tr in next sp, tr in next tr, ch 3, sk 3 tr, tr in next tr, 3 tr in next sp, (ch 3, tr in next tr) 4 times, (ch 3, sk 3 tr, tr in next tr) 7 times, ch 3, * tr, ch 7, tr in 4th ch of corner sp, ch 3, tr in next tr, (ch 3, sk 3 tr, tr in next tr) 7 times, (ch 3, tr in next tr) 4 times, (3 tr in next sp, tr in next tr, ch 3, sk 3 tr, tr in next tr) twice, 3 tr in next sp, tr in next tr, (ch 3, tr in next tr) 4 times, (ch 3, sk 3 tr, tr in next tr) 7 times, ch 3, repeat from * twice, tr, ch 7, tr in 4th ch of corner sp, ch 3, tr in next tr, (ch 3, sk 3 tr, tr in next tr) 7 times, (ch 3, tr in next tr) 4 times, 3 tr in next sp, tr in next tr, ch 3, sl st in top of ch-4.

Rnd 16: Ch 7, sk 3 tr, tr in next tr, 3 tr in next sp, tr in next tr, ch 3, sk 3 tr, tr in next tr, 3 tr in next sp, tr in next tr, (ch 3, tr in next tr) 7 times, (3 tr in next sp, tr in next tr) 4 times, * 4 tr, ch 7, 4 tr in corner sp, tr in next tr, (3 tr in next sp, tr in next tr) 4 times, (ch 3, tr in next tr) 7 times, (3 tr in next sp, tr in next tr, ch 3, sk 3 tr, tr in next tr) 3 times, 3 tr in next sp, tr in next tr, (ch 3, tr in next tr) 7 times, (3 tr in next sp, tr in next tr) 4 times, repeat from * twice, 4 tr, ch 7, 4 tr in corner sp, tr in next tr, (3 tr in next sp, tr in next tr) 4 times, (ch 3, tr in next tr) 7 times, 3 tr in next sp, tr in next tr, ch 3, sk 3 tr, tr in next tr, 3 tr in last sp, sl st in 4th ch of ch-7.

Rnd 17: Ch 4, (3 tr in next sp, tr in next tr, ch 3, sk 3 tr, tr in next tr) twice, 3 tr in next sp, tr in next tr, (ch 3, tr in next tr) 5 times, 3 tr in next sp, tr in each of 21 tr, * 4 tr, ch 7, 4 tr in corner sp, tr in each of 21 tr, 3 tr in next sp, tr in next tr, (ch 3, tr in next tr) 5 times, (3 tr in next sp, tr in next tr, ch 3, sk 3 tr, tr in next tr) 4 times, 3 tr in next sp, tr in next tr, (ch 3, tr in next tr) 5 times, 3 tr in next sp, tr in each of 21 tr, repeat from * twice, 4 tr, ch 7, 4 tr in corner sp, tr in each of 21 tr, 3 tr in next sp, tr in next tr, (ch 3, tr in next tr) 5 times, 3 tr in next sp, tr in next tr, ch 3, sk 3 tr, tr in next tr, 3 tr in next sp, tr in next tr, ch 3, sl st in top of ch-4.

Rnd 18: Ch 7, sk 3 tr, tr in next tr, (3 tr in next sp, tr in next tr, ch 3, sk 3 tr, tr in next tr) twice, 3 tr in next sp, tr in next tr, (ch 3, tr in next tr) 4 times, (ch 3, sk 3 tr, tr in next tr) 7 times, ch 3, * tr, ch 7, tr in 4th ch of corner sp, ch 3, tr in next tr, (ch 3, sk 3 tr, tr in next tr) 7 times, (ch 3, tr in next tr) 4 times, (3 tr in next sp, tr in next tr, ch 3, sk 3 tr, tr in next tr) 5 times, 3 tr in next sp, tr in next tr, (ch 3, tr in next tr) 4 times, (ch 3, sk 3 tr, tr in next tr) 7 times, ch 3, repeat from * twice, tr, ch 7, tr in 4th ch of corner sp, ch 3, tr in next tr, (ch 3, sk 3 tr, tr in next tr) 7 times, (ch 3, tr in next tr) 4 times, (3 tr in next sp, tr in next tr, ch 3, sk 3 tr, tr in next tr) twice, 3 tr in next sp, sl st in 4th ch of ch-7.

Rnd 19: Ch 4, (3 tr in next sp, tr in next tr, ch 3, sk 3 tr, tr in next tr) 3 times, 3 tr in next sp, tr in next tr, (ch 3, tr in next tr) 7 times, (3 tr in next sp, tr in next tr) 4 times, * 4 tr, ch 7, 4 tr in corner sp, tr in next tr, (3 tr in next sp, tr in next tr) 4 times, (ch 3, tr in next tr) 7 times, (3 tr in next sp, tr in next tr, ch 3, sk 3 tr, tr in next tr) 6 times, 3 tr in next sp, tr in next tr, (ch 3, tr in next tr) 7 times, (3 tr in next sp, tr in next tr) 4 times, repeat from * twice, 4 tr, ch 7, 4 tr in corner sp, tr in next tr, (3 tr in next sp, tr in next tr) 4 times, (ch 3, tr in next tr) 7 times, (3 tr in next sp, tr in next tr, ch 3, sk 3 tr, tr in next tr) twice, 3 tr in next sp, tr in next tr, ch 3, sl st in top of ch-4.

Rnd 20: Ch 7, sk 3 tr, tr in next tr, (3 tr in next sp, tr in next tr, ch 3, sk 3 tr, tr in next tr) 3 times, 3 tr in next sp, tr in next tr, (ch 3, tr in next tr) 5 times, 3 tr in next sp, tr in each of 21 tr, * 4 tr, ch 7, 4 tr in corner sp, tr in each of 21 tr, 3 tr in next sp, tr in next tr, (ch 3, tr in next tr) 5 times, (3 tr in next sp, tr in next tr, ch 3, sk 3 tr, tr in next tr) 7 times, 3 tr in next sp, tr in next tr, (ch 3, tr in next tr) 5 times, 3 tr in next sp, tr in each of 21 tr, repeat from * twice, 4 tr, ch 7, 4 tr in corner sp, tr in each of 21 tr, 3 tr in next sp, tr in next tr, (ch 3, tr in next tr) 5 times, (3 tr in next sp, tr in next tr, ch 3, sk 3 tr, tr in next tr) 3 times, 3 tr in next sp, sl st in 4th ch of ch-7. End off.

Make bedspread 5 squares wide by 6 squares long, joining squares tog on last rnd as follows:

Rnd 20: Work as for first square to first corner, 4 tr in corner sp, ch 3, drop lp off hook, insert hook in 4th ch of ch 7 of previous square, draw dropped lp through, ch 3, (tr in corner sp, drop lp from hook, insert hook in top of corresponding tr of previous square, draw dropped lp through) 4 times, tr in each of 21 tr, joining each tr to corresponding tr in same way, 3 tr in next sp and tr in next tr, joining each tr to corresponding tr in same way, (ch 3, tr in next tr, join to corresponding tr) 5 times, continue across to next corner, joining each tr to corresponding tr of previous square, join 2nd corner same as first corner was joined, then finish rnd as for first square.

BORDER: When all squares have been joined, join thread in 4th ch of corner sp at any corner of bedspread.

Rnd 1: Ch 11, tr in same ch of corner sp as joining, * ch 3, tr in next tr, (ch 3, sk 3 tr, tr in next tr) 7 times, (ch 3, tr in next tr) 5 times, (ch 3, sk 3 tr, tr in next tr, ch 3, tr in next tr) 7 times, ch 3, sk 3 tr, tr in next tr, (ch 3, tr in next tr) 5 times, (ch 3, sk 3 tr, tr in next tr) 7 times, ch 3, tr in joining of squares, repeat from * across one side of bedspread, end ch 3, tr, ch 7, tr in 4th ch of corner sp, repeat from first * around bedspread, end last repeat ch 3, sl st in 4th ch of ch-11.

Rnd 2: Sl st in corner sp, ch 4 for first tr, 15 tr in corner sp, * ch 4, sk 1 sp, sc in next sp, ch 4, sk 1 sp, 9 tr in next sp, repeat from * across one side of bedspread, ch 4, sk 1 sp, sc in next sp, ch 4, 16 tr in corner sp, repeat from first * around bedspread, end last repeat ch 4, sl st in top of first tr.

Rnd 3: Ch 8, sc in 4th ch from hook for picot, (tr in next tr, ch 4, sc in 4th ch from hook for picot) 14 times, tr in next tr, * ch 3, sc in sc, ch 3, tr, picot in each of next 8 tr, tr in 9th tr, repeat from * across one side of bedspread, ch 3, sc in sc, ch 3, tr, picot in each of 15 tr, tr in 16th tr, repeat from first * around bedspread, end last repeat ch 3, sl st in 4th ch of ch-8. End off.

FILET SQUARE PILLOWS

SIZE: 16″ square, plus shell edging.
MATERIALS: DMC Cébélia Fil d'Ecosse, size 10, two 282-yard balls white for each pillow. Steel crochet hook No. 8 (1.25 mm) or size required to obtain gauge. Fabric, 1¼ yards for each pillow. 16″ pillow form.
GAUGE: 21 tr = 2″; 3 rows = 1″.

PILLOW A

Beg at center of pillow, ch 6. Sl st in first ch to form ring. Work same as bedspread square through rnd 19.

Rnd 20: Ch 7, sk 3 tr, tr in next tr, (3 tr in next sp, tr in next tr, ch 3, sk 3 tr, tr in next tr) 3 times, (ch 3, tr in next tr) 6 times, 3 tr in next sp, tr in each of next 21 tr, * 4 tr, ch 7, 4 tr in corner sp, tr in each of next 21 tr, 3 tr in next sp, tr in next tr, (ch 3, tr in next tr) 6 times, (ch 3, sk 3 tr, tr in next tr, 3 tr in next sp, tr in next tr) 6 times, ch 3, sk 3 tr, tr in next tr, (ch 3, tr in next tr) 6 times, 3 tr in next sp, tr in each of next 21 tr, repeat from * twice, 4 tr, ch 7, 4 tr in corner sp, tr in each of next 21 tr, 3 tr in next sp, tr in next tr, (ch 3, tr in next tr) 6 times, (ch 3, sk 3 tr, tr in next tr, 3 tr in next sp, tr in next tr) twice, ch 3, sk 3 tr, tr in next tr, 3 tr in last sp, sl st in top of ch-4.

Rnd 21: Ch 4, 3 tr in first sp, tr in next tr, (ch 3, sk 3 tr, tr in next tr, 3 tr in next sp, tr in next tr) twice, ch 3, sk 3 tr, tr in next tr, (ch 3, tr in next tr) 7 times, (ch 3, sk 3 tr, tr in next tr) 7 times, ch 3, * tr, ch 7, tr in 4th ch of corner sp, ch 3, tr in next tr, (ch 3, sk 3 tr, tr in next tr) 7 times, (ch 3, tr in next tr) 7 times, (ch 3, sk 3 tr, tr in next tr, 3 tr in next sp, tr in next tr) 5 times, ch 3, sk 3 tr, tr in next tr, (ch 3, tr in next tr) 7 times, (ch 3, sk 3 tr, tr in next tr) 7 times, ch 3, repeat from * twice, tr, ch 7, tr in 4th ch of corner sp, ch 3, tr in next tr, (ch 3, sk 3 tr, tr in next tr) 7 times, (ch 3, tr in next tr) 7 times, (ch 3, sk 3 tr, tr in next tr, 3 tr in next sp, tr in next tr) twice, ch 3, sl st in top of ch-4.

Rnd 22: Ch 7, sk 3 tr, tr in next tr, (3 tr in next sp, tr in next tr, ch 3, sk 3 tr, tr in next tr) twice, (ch 3, tr in next tr) 12 times, (3 tr in next sp, tr in next tr) 4 times, * 4 tr, ch 7, 4 tr in corner sp, tr in next tr, (3 tr in next sp, tr in next tr) 4 times, (ch 3, tr in next tr) 12 times, (ch 3, sk 3 tr, tr in next tr, 3 tr in next sp, tr in next tr) 4 times, ch 3, sk 3 tr, tr in next tr, (ch 3, tr in next tr) 12 times, (3 tr in next sp, tr in next tr) 4 times, repeat from * twice, 4 tr, ch 7, 4 tr in corner sp, tr in next tr, (3 tr in next sp, tr in next tr) 4 times, (ch 3, tr in next tr) 12 times, ch 3, sk 3 tr, tr in next tr, 3 tr in next sp, tr in next tr, ch 3, sk 3 tr, tr in next tr, 3 tr in last sp, sl st in 4th ch of ch-7.

Rnd 23: Ch 4, (3 tr in next sp, tr in next tr, ch 3, sk 3 tr, tr in next tr) twice, (ch 3, tr in next tr) 12 times, 3 tr in next sp, tr in each of next 21 tr, * 4 tr, ch 7, 4 tr in corner sp, tr in each of next 21 tr, 3 tr in next sp, tr in next tr, (ch 3, tr in next tr) 12 times, (ch 3, sk 3 tr, tr in next tr, 3 tr in next sp, tr in next tr) 3 times, ch 3, sk 3 tr, tr in next tr, (ch 3, tr in next tr) 12 times, 3 tr in next sp, tr in each of next 21 tr, repeat from * twice, 4 tr, ch 7, 4 tr in corner sp, tr in each of next 21 tr, 3 tr in next sp, tr in next tr, (ch 3, tr in next tr) 12 times, ch 3, sk 3 tr, tr in next tr, 3 tr in next sp, tr in next tr, ch 3, sl st in top of ch-4.

Rnd 24: Ch 7, sk 3 tr, tr in next tr, 3 tr in next sp, tr in next tr, ch 3, sk 3 tr, tr in next tr, (ch 3, tr in next tr) 13 times, (ch 3, sk 3 tr, tr in next tr) 7 times, ch 3, * tr, ch 7, tr in 4th ch of corner sp, ch 3, tr in next tr, (ch 3, sk 3 tr, tr in next tr) 7 times, (ch 3, tr in next tr) 13 times, (ch 3, sk 3 tr, tr in next tr, 3 tr in next sp, tr in next tr) twice, ch 3, sk 3 tr, tr in next tr, (ch 3, tr in next tr) 13 times, (ch 3, sk 3 tr, tr in next tr) 7 times, ch 3, repeat from * twice, tr, ch 7, tr in 4th ch of corner sp, ch 3, tr in next tr, (ch 3, sk 3 tr, tr in next tr) 7 times, (ch 3, tr in next tr) 13 times, ch 3, sk 3 tr, tr in next tr, 3 tr in last sp, sl st in 4th ch of ch-7.

Rnd 25: Ch 4 for first tr, 9 tr in next sp, ch 4, sc in next sp, (ch 4, sk 1 sp, 10 tr in next sp, ch 4, sk 1 sp, sc in next sp) 5 times, ch 4, * 15 tr in corner sp, ch 4, sk 1 sp, sc in next sp, (ch 4, sk 1 sp, 10 tr in next sp, ch 4, sk 1 sp, sc in next sp) 5 times, ch 4, 10 tr in next sp, ch 4, sc in next sp, (ch 4, sk 1 sp, 10 tr in next sp, ch 4, sk 1 sp, sc in next sp) 5 times, ch 4, repeat from * twice, 15 tr in corner sp, ch 4, sk 1 sp, sc in next sp, (ch 4, sk 1 sp, 10 tr in next sp, ch 4, sk 1 sp, sc in next sp) 5 times, ch 4, sl st in top of first tr.

Rnd 26: Ch 8, sc in 4th ch from hook for picot, (tr in next tr, ch 4, sc in 4th ch from hook for picot) 8 times, tr in next tr, * ch 3, sc in sc, ch 3, tr, picot in each of next 9 tr, tr in next tr, repeat from * around, working tr, picot in each of 14 tr at corners, end sl st in 4th ch of ch-8. End off.

PILLOW B

Work as for Pillow A through rnd 9.

Rnd 10: Ch 4, 3 tr in next sp, tr in next tr, (ch 3, tr in next tr) 6 times, (3 tr in next sp, tr in next tr) twice, * 4 tr, ch 7, 4 tr in corner sp, tr in next tr, (3 tr in next sp, tr in next tr) twice, (ch 3, tr in next tr) 6 times, 3 tr in next sp, tr in next tr, (ch 3, tr in next tr) 6 times, (3 tr in next sp, tr in next tr) twice, repeat from * twice, 4 tr, ch 7, 4 tr in corner sp, tr in next tr, (3 tr in next sp, tr in next tr) twice, (ch 3, tr in next tr) 5 times, ch 3, sl st in top of ch-4.

Rnd 11: Ch 7, sk 3 tr, tr in next tr, 3 tr in next sp, tr in next tr, (ch 3, tr in next tr) 4 times, 3 tr in next sp, tr in each of next 13 tr, * 4tr, ch 7, 4 tr in corner sp, tr in each of next 13 tr, 3 tr in next sp, tr in next tr, (ch 3, tr in next tr) 4 times, 3 tr in next sp, tr in next tr, ch 3, sk 3 tr, tr in next tr, 3 tr in next sp, tr in next tr, (ch 3, tr in next tr) 4 times, 3 tr in next sp, tr in each of next 13 tr, repeat from * twice, 4 tr, ch 7, 4 tr in corner sp, tr in each of next 13 tr, 3 tr in next sp, tr in next tr, (ch 3, tr in next tr) 4 times, 3 tr in last sp, sl st in 4th ch of ch-7.

Rnd 12: Ch 4, 3 tr in next sp, tr in next tr, ch 3, sk 3 tr, tr in next tr, 3 tr in next sp, tr in next tr, (ch 3, tr in next tr) 3 times, (ch 3, sk 3 tr, tr in next tr) 5 times, ch 3, * tr, ch 7, tr in 4th ch of corner sp, ch 3, tr in next tr, (ch 3, sk 3 tr, tr in next tr) 5 times, (ch 3, tr in next tr) 3 tmes, (3 tr in next sp, tr in next tr, ch 3, sk 3 tr, tr in next tr) twice, 3 tr in next sp, tr in next tr, (ch 3, tr in next tr) 3 times, (ch 3, sk 3 tr, tr in in next tr) 5 times, ch 3, repeat from * twice, tr, ch 7, tr in 4th ch of corner sp, ch 3, tr in next tr, (ch 3, sk 3 tr, tr in next tr) 5 times, (ch 3, tr in next tr) 3 times, 3 tr in next sp, tr in next tr, ch 3, sl st in top of ch-4.

Rnd 13: Ch 7, sk 3 tr, tr in next tr, 3 tr in next sp, tr in next tr, ch 3, sk 3 tr, tr in next tr, 3 tr in next sp, tr in next tr, (ch 3, tr in next tr) 5 times, (3 tr in next sp, tr in next tr) 3 times, * 4 tr, ch 7, 4 tr in corner sp, tr in next tr, (3 tr in next sp, tr in next tr) 3 times, (ch 3, tr in next tr) 5 times, (3 tr in next tr, ch 3, sk 3 tr, tr in next tr) 3 times, 3 tr in next sp, tr in next tr, (ch 3, tr in next tr) 5 times, (3 tr in next sp, tr in next tr) 3 times, repeat from * twice, 4 tr, ch 7, 4 tr in corner sp, tr in next tr, (3 tr in next sp, tr in next tr) 3 times, (ch 3, tr in next tr) 5 times, 3 tr in next sp, tr in next tr, ch 3, sk 3 tr, tr in next tr, 3 tr in next sp, sl st in 4th ch of ch-7.

For ease in reading directions, from this point on, each space of ch 3, tr will be called 1 sp and each block of 3 tr, tr will be called 1 bl.

Rnd 14: Ch 4, 1 bl, 1 sp, 1 bl, 1 sp, 1 bl, 3 sps, 5bls, * 4 tr, ch 7, 4 tr in corner sp, tr in next tr, 5 bls, 3 sps, (1 bl, 1 sp) 4 times, 1 bl, 3 sps, 5 bls, repeat from * twice, 4 tr, ch 7, 4 tr in corner sp, tr in next tr, 5 bls, 3 sps, 1 bl, 1 sp, 1 bl, ch 3, sl st in top of ch-4.

Rnd 15: Ch 7, sk 3 tr, tr in next tr, (1 bl, 1 sp) twice, 1 bl, 8 sps, ch 3, * tr, ch 7, tr in 4th ch of corner sp, ch 3, tr in next tr, 8 sps, (1 bl, 1 sp) 5 times, 1 bl, 8 sps, ch 3, repeat from * twice, tr, ch 7, tr in 4th ch of corner sp, ch 3, tr in next tr, 8 sps, (1 bl, 1 sp) twice, 3 tr in last sp, sl st in 4th ch of ch-7.

Rnd 16: Ch 4, (1 bl, 1 sp) twice, 1 bl, 6 sps, 4 bls, * 4 tr, ch 7, 4 tr in corner sp, tr in next tr, 4 bls, 6 sps, (1 bl, 1 sp) 4 times, 1 bl, 6 sps, 4 bls, repeat from * twice, 4 tr, ch 7, 4 tr in corner sp, tr in next tr, 4 bls, 6 sps, 1 bl, 1 sp, 1 bl, ch 3, sl st in top of ch-4.

Rnd 17: Ch 7, sk 3 tr, tr in next tr, 1 bl, 1 sp, 1 bl, 6 sps, 6 bls, * 4 tr, ch 7, 4 tr in corner sp, tr in next tr, 6 bls, 6 sps, (1 bl, 1 sp) 3 times, 1 bl, 6 sps, 6 bls, repeat from * twice, 4 tr, ch 7, 4 tr in corner sp, tr in next tr, 6 bls, 6 sps, 1 bl, 1 sp, 3 tr in last sp, sl st in 4th ch of ch-7.

Rnd 18: Ch 4, 1 bl, 1 sp, 1 bl, 14 sps, ch 3, * tr, ch 7, tr in 4th ch of corner sp, ch 3, tr in next tr, 14 sps, (1 bl, 1 sp) twice, 1 bl, 14 sps, ch 3, repeat from * twice, tr, ch 7, tr in 4th ch of corner sp, ch 3, tr in next tr, 14 sps, 1 bl, ch 3, sl st in top of ch-4.

Rnd 19: Ch 7, sk 3 tr, tr in next tr, 1 bl, 12 sps, 4 bls, * 4 tr, ch 7, 4 tr in corner sp, tr in next tr, 4 bls, 12 sps, 1 bl, 1 sp, 1 bl, 12 sps, 4 bls, repeat from * twice, 4 tr, ch 7, 4 tr in corner sp, tr in next tr, 4 bls, 12 sps, 3 tr in last sp, sl st in 4th ch of ch-7.

Rnd 20: Ch 4, 1 bl, 12 sps, 6 bls, * 4 tr, ch 7, 4 tr in corner sp, tr in next tr, 6 bls, 12 sps, 1 bl, 12 sps, 6 bls, repeat from * twice, 4 tr, ch 7, 4 tr in corner sp, tr in next tr, 6 bls, 11 sps, ch 3, sl st in top of ch-4.

Rnd 21: Ch 7, sk 3 tr, tr in next tr, 6 sps, 1 bl, 12 sps, ch 3, * tr, ch 7, tr in 4th ch of corner sp, ch 3, tr in next tr, 12 sps, 1 bl, 13 sps, 1 bl, 12 sps, ch 3, repeat from * twice, tr, ch 7, tr in 4th ch of corner sp, ch 3, tr in next tr, 12 sps, 1 bl, 5 sps, ch 3, sl st in 4th ch of ch-7.

Rnd 22: Ch 7, tr in next tr, 5 sps, 1 bl, 1 sp, 1 bl, 12 sps, ch 3, * tr, ch 7, tr in 4th ch of corner sp, ch 3, tr in next tr, 12 sps, 1 bl, 1 sp, 1 bl, 11 sps, 1 bl, 1 sp, 1 bl, 12 sps, ch 3, repeat from * twice, tr, ch 7, tr in 4th ch of corner sp, ch 3, tr in next tr, 12 sps, 1 bl, 1 sp, 1 bl, 4 sps, ch 3, sl st in 4th ch of ch-7.

Rnd 23: Ch 7, tr in next tr, 6 sps, 1 bl, 14 sps, ch 3, * tr, ch 7, tr in 4th ch of corner sp, ch 3, tr in next tr, 14 sps, 1 bl, 13 sps, 1 bl, 14 sps, ch 3, repeat from * twice, tr, ch 7, tr in 4th ch of corner sp, ch 3, tr in next tr, 14 sps, 1 bl, 5 sps, ch 3, sl st in 4th ch of ch-7.

Rnd 24: Ch 4, 7 tr in first sp, ch 3, sk 1 sp, sc in next sp, ch 3, sk 1 sp, 8 tr in next sp, ch 3, sk 1 sp, sc in next sp, ch 3, sk 1 bl, 8 tr in next sp, (ch 3, sk 1 sp, sc in next sp, ch 3, sk 1 sp, 8 tr in next sp) 3 times, ch 3, sk 1 sp, sc in next sp, ch 3, * 12 tr in corner sp, ch 3, sc in next sp, (ch 3, sk 1 sp, 8 tr in next sp, ch 3, sk 1 sp, sc in next sp) 3 times, ch 3, sk 1 sp, 8 tr in next sp, ch 3, sk 1 bl, sc in next sp, (ch 3, sk 1 sp, 8 tr in next sp, ch 3, sk 1 sp, sc in next sp) 3 times, ch 3, sk 1 bl, 8 tr in next sp, (ch 3, sk 1 sp, sc in next sp, ch 3, sk 1 sp, 8 tr in next sp) 3 times, ch 3, sk 1 sp, sc in next sp, ch 3, repeat from * twice, 12 tr in corner sp, ch 3, sc in next sp, (ch 3, sk 1 sp, 8 tr in next sp, ch 3, sk 1 sp, sc in next sp) 3 times, ch 3, sk 1 sp, 8 tr in next sp, ch 3, sk 1 bl, sc in next sp, ch 3, sk 1 sp, 8 tr in next sp, ch 3, sk 1 bl, sc in next sp, ch 3, sl st in top of ch-4.

Rnd 25: Ch 5, (tr in next tr, ch 1) 6 times, tr in next tr, (ch 2, sc in next sc, ch 2, tr, ch 1 in each of next 7 tr, tr in next tr) 5 times, * ch 2, tr, ch 1 in each of next 11 tr, tr in next tr, (ch 2, sc in next sc, ch 2, tr, ch 1 in each of next 7 tr, tr in next tr) 11 times, ch 2, sc in next sc, repeat from * twice, ch 2, tr, ch 1 in each of next 11 tr, tr in next tr, (ch 2, sc in next sc, ch 2, tr, ch 1 in each of next 7 tr, tr in next tr) 5 times, ch 2, sc in next sc, ch 2, sl st in 4th ch of ch-5.

Rnd 26: Ch 8, sc in 4th ch from hook for picot, (tr in next tr, ch 4, sc in 4th sc from hook for picot) 6 times, tr in next tr, (ch 2, sc in next sc, ch 2, tr, picot in each of next 7 tr, tr in next tr) 5 times, ch 2, sc in next sc, * ch 2, tr, picot in each of next 11 tr, tr in next tr, (ch 2, sc in next sc, ch 2, tr, picot in each of next 7 tr, tr in next tr) 11 times, ch 2, sc in next sc, repeat from * twice, ch 2, tr, picot in each of 11 tr, tr in next tr, (ch 2, sc in next sc, ch 2, tr, picot in each of next 7 tr, tr in next tr) 5 times, ch 2, sc in next sc, ch 2, sl st in top of ch-4. End off.

FINISHING: Cut two pieces of fabric 17″ square. Cut 4¼″-wide strips and join for a 160″-long ruffle strip. Stitch ends of ruffle pieces together, forming a ring. With right side out, fold piece in half lengthwise, bringing raw edges together; press well. Gather piece ½″ from raw edges. Pin ruffle to right side of front fabric square, matching raw edges and placing gathers evenly; stitch around fabric square with ½″ seam. Pin pillow front and back tog with right sides facing; stitch around three sides with ½″ seam. Turn to right side; insert pillow form and close opening. Sew crocheted pillow top to pillow, stitching base of shell edging to bottom of ruffle.

LONG FILET SQUARE PILLOW

SIZE: 18″ × 33″.
MATERIALS: DMC Cébélia Fil d'Ecosse, size 10, four 282-yard balls white. Steel crochet hook No. 7 (1.5 mm) or size required to obtain gauge. Fabric, 2 yards. Stuffing.
GAUGE: 10 tr = 1″; 8 rnds = 3″. Each motif is 15″ square.
PILLOW: FIRST SQUARE: Work as for first square of bedspread. Make another square and join to first square as bedspread squares were joined.
BORDER: Rnd 1: Join thread in 4th ch of corner sp at beg of long side of pillow. Ch 11, tr in same ch as joining, * ch 3, tr in next tr, (ch 3, sk 3 tr, tr in next tr) 7 times, (ch 3, tr in next tr) 5 times, (ch 3, sk 3 tr, tr in next tr, ch 3, tr in next tr) 7 times, ch 3, sk 3 tr, tr in next tr, (ch 3, tr in next tr) 5 times, (ch 3, sk 3 tr, tr in next tr) 7 times, * ch 3, tr in joining of squares, repeat from first * to 2nd * across next square, end ch 3, tr, ch 7, tr in 4th ch of corner sp, repeat from first * to 2nd * across short end of pillow, end ch 3, tr, ch 7, tr in 4th ch of corner sp, repeat from first * across long side and short end, end ch 3, sl st in 4th ch of beg ch-11.

Rnd 2: Sl st in corner sp, ch 4 for first tr, 16 tr in corner sp, * ch 3, sc in next sp, ch 3, sk 1 sp, 11 tr in next sp, ch 3, sk 1 sp, sc in next sp, repeat from * across one side, ch 3, 17 tr in corner sp, repeat from * around, end ch 3, sl st in top of ch-4.
Rnd 3: Ch 5, (tr in next tr, ch 1) 15 times, tr in next tr, * ch 3, sc in sc, ch 3, (tr in next tr, ch 1) 10 times, tr in next tr, repeat from * across one side, ch 3, sc in sc, ch 3, (tr in next tr, ch 1) 16 times, tr in next tr, repeat from first * around, end ch 3, sl st in 4th ch of ch-5.
Rnd 4: Ch 8, sc in 4th ch from hook for picot, (tr in next tr, ch 4, sc in 4th sc from hook for picot) 15 times, tr in next tr, * ch 2, sc in next sc, ch 2, tr, picot in each of next 10 tr, tr in next tr, repeat from * across one side, ch 2, sc in next sc, ch 2, tr, picot in each of next 16 tr, tr in next tr, repeat from first * around, end ch 2, sl st in 4th ch of ch-8. End off.
FINISHING: Cut two pieces of fabric 34″ × 19″. Cut 4½″-wide strips and join for a 208″-long ruffle. Complete pillow as for Filet Square Pillows, stuffing firmly before closing last seam.

FILET SQUARE TABLECLOTH

SIZE: 32″ square.
MATERIALS: DMC Cébélia Fil d'Ecosse, size 10, six 282-yard balls white. Steel crochet hook No. 8 (1.25 mm) or size required to obtain gauge.
GAUGE: 21 tr = 2″; 3 rows = 1″. Each motif is 14″ square.
TABLECLOTH: FIRST SQUARE: Work as for bedspread square. Make tablecloth 2 squares by 2 squares, joining squares tog on last rnd as bedspread squares were joined. Work border same as bedspread.

Fancy 'n' Feminine

Traditional and romantic-looking accessories for the boudoir make beautiful gifts for a lucky bride-to-be. It takes little time to create these lovely items, and the hanger covers and lacy crocheted collar are great projects for beginners.

PILLOWCASE EDGINGS

SIZE: Fits standard-size pillowcase.
MATERIALS (for each edging): Pearl cotton size 5, three 25-meter (27.3-yard) skeins pink, blue, or green. Crochet hooks sizes 2/C and 3/D (2.75 and 3.25 mm) or size required to obtain gauge. Satin ribbon ¼″ wide, 1¼ yards. Matching sewing thread.

PINK EDGING

GAUGE: 28 sts = 4″.
EDGING: With smaller hook, ch 306.
Row 1: Sc in 2nd ch from hook and in each ch across—305 sc. Ch 6, turn.

Row 2 (beading row): Hdc in 5th sc, *ch 3, sk 3 sc, hdc in next sc, repeat from * across. Ch 3, turn.

Row 3: Sc in 2nd ch of ch-3 sp, * ch 4, sc in next ch-3 sp, repeat from * across, end ch 1, sc in 5th ch of ch-6, ch 1, hdc in 3rd ch of same ch-6. Ch 1, turn.

Row 4: Sc in hdc, * ch 4, sc in next ch-4 sp, repeat from * across, end ch 4, sc in 2nd ch of ch-3. Ch 6, turn.

Row 5: Repeat row 3, working sc in ch-4 sp.

Rows 6 and 8: Sc in hdc, * sc in next sc, 3 sc in ch-4 sp, repeat from * across, end sc in top of ch-3.

Row 7: Sc in sc, * ch 4, sk 3 sc, sc in next sc, repeat from * across. Ch 1, turn.

Row 9: Sl st in first 2 sc, * ch 4, sk 1 sc, sl st in next 3 sc, repeat from * across, end last repeat sl st in last 2 sc. End off.

FINISHING: Block to fit around pillowcase. Weave satin ribbon over and under hdc's of beading row; overlap and tack short ends of ribbon together.

Sew edging around right side of pillowcase above and below beading row. Tie two small bows along front of beading row.

BLUE EDGING

GAUGE: 22 sts = 4″.

EDGING: With larger hook, ch 238.

Row 1: Sc in 2nd ch from hook and in each ch across—237 sc. Ch 6, turn.

Row 2 (beading row): Hdc in 5th sc, * ch 3, sk 3 sc, hdc in next sc, repeat from * across. Ch 1, turn.

Row 3: * Sc in hdc, 3 sc in ch-3 sp, dec 7 sc evenly spaced across, end 2 sc in top of ch-6. Ch 5, turn.

Row 4: * (2 dc, ch 1, 2 dc) in next sc—large shell made, sk 2 sc (dc, ch 1, dc) in next sc—small shell made, sk 2 sc, repeat from * across, end dc in last sc.

Row 5: Ch 3, * large shell in ch-1 sp of large shell, small shell in ch-1 sp of small shell, repeat from * across, end dc in top of ch-5.

Row 6: Ch 3, * (2 dc, ch 2, 2 dc) in ch-1 sp of large shell, small shell in ch-1 sp of small shell, repeat from * across.

Rows 7–10: Repeat row 6, working one more ch each row in sp of large shells. End off.

FINISHING: Work same as pink edging.

Green Edging

GAUGE: 24 sts = 4".
EDGING: With smaller hook, ch 258.
Row 1: Sc in 2nd ch from hook and in each ch across—257 sc. Ch 3, turn.
Row 2: * Sk 2 sc (dc, ch 1, dc) in next sc, repeat from * across to last 2 sc, sk 1 sc, dc in last sc.
Row 3: * Ch 5, sc in ch-1 sp, repeat from * across, end ch 2, dc in top of ch-3.
Row 4: Ch 3, 3 dc in ch-2 sp, * (sc in ch-5 sp, ch 5) 3 times, sc in ch-5 sp, 7 dc in next ch-5 sp, repeat from * across, end last repeat 4 dc in last ch-5 sp.
Row 5: Ch 4, sc in 2nd dc, (ch 1, dc in next dc) twice, * (ch 1, sc in ch-5 sp, ch 5) twice, sc in ch-5 sp, (ch 1, dc in next dc) 7 times, repeat from * across, end last repeat (ch 1, dc in dc) 3 times, ch 1, dc in top of ch-3.
Row 6: Ch 5, dc in 2nd dc, (ch 2, dc in next dc) twice, * ch 2, sc in ch-5 sp, ch 5, sc in next ch-5 sp, (ch 2, dc in next dc) 7 times, repeat from * across, end (ch 2, dc in next dc) 3 times, ch 2, dc in 3rd ch of ch-4.
Row 7: (Ch 3, sc in first ch—picot made) 4 times, * picot, sc in ch-3 sp, (picot, dc in ch-2 sp) 8 times, repeat from * across, end (picot, dc in ch-2 sp) 5 times. End off.
FINISHING: Work same as pink edging.

Wedding Day Hankies

SIZE: Edged handkerchief, 11" square.
MATERIALS: Crochet cotton size 30, one ball white. Steel crochet hook No. 14. Linen handkerchiefs, 10" square with hemstitched edges.
CLUSTER EDGING: Rnd 1: Beg at one corner of handkerchief, sc in each hemstitched hole, working 3 sc in each corner. Sl st in first sc. Ch 3.
Rnd 2: Holding back last lp of each dc, work 2 dc in base of ch-3, yo and pull through 3 lps on hook—beg cluster made, * holding back last lp of each dc, work 3 dc in next sc, yo and pull through 4 lps on hook—3-dc cluster made, ch 3, 3-dc cluster in same dc, sk 4 dc, repeat from * to last sc before next corner, spacing skipped sc's to fit, 3-dc cluster, ch 3, 3-dc cluster in corner, repeat from * around handkerchief to last corner, 3-dc cluster in corner, ch 3, sl st in top of beg cluster.
Rnd 3: Beg cluster in ch-2 sp of first corner, * ch 8, sl st in 6th ch from hook for picot, ch 2, 3-dc cluster in next ch-3 sp, repeat from * around, working 3-dc cluster, ch 8, picot, 3-dc cluster in each corner, end sl st in top of beg cluster. End off.
CROSS-STITCH EDGING: Rnd 1: Beg at one corner of handkerchief, sc in each hemstitched hole, working 3 sc in each corner, sl st in first sc. Ch 3.

Rnd 2: Yo twice, pull up a lp in base of ch-3, yo and pull through 2 lps on hook, sk 3 sc, yo and pull up a lp in next sc, * (yo and pull through 2 lps on hook) 4 times, ch 3, dc in center of cross-stitch, yo twice, pull up a lp in same sc where last cross-stitch ended, repeat from * around handkerchief, skipping sc's as necessary to have a cross-stitch in each corner. Sl st to top of beg ch-3, sl st in first ch-3 sp.
Rnd 3: Ch 2, 2 hdc, ch 5, sl st in 4th ch from hook for picot, * ch 1, 3 hdc in next ch-3 sp, ch 5, picot, repeat from * around, sl st in top of beg ch. End off.

Tasseled Pomanders

SIZE: 2½" diameter.
MATERIALS: Fingering weight cotton yarn, one 50-gram (1.75-oz.) ball white. Six-strand embroidery floss, one skein each red (A), dark pink (B), melon (C), bright green (D), medium pink (E), mauve (F), blue-green (G), mint green (H). Pearl cotton size 3, one skein each pink, blue, green for tassels. Crochet hooks sizes 2/C and 5/F (2.75 and 3.75 mm) or size required to obtain gauge. Satin ribbon ¼" wide, 6" for each sachet. Potpourri. Large-eyed tapestry needle. Twenty-four 3-mm gold plated beads.
GAUGE: 20 sc = 4" (larger hook); 24 rows = 4".
SACHET: With cotton yarn and larger hook, ch 4. Sl st in first ch to form ring.
Rnd 1: 10 sc in ring. Do not join; mark first sc each rnd.
Rnd 2: Sc around, inc 6 sc evenly spaced—16 sc.
Rnd 3: Sc around, inc 8 sc evenly spaced—24 sc.
Rnds 4 and 5: Sc around.
Rnd 6: Sc around, inc 8 sc evenly spaced—32 sc.
Rnd 7: Sc around.
Rnd 8: Sc around, inc 8 sc evenly spaced—40 sc.
Rnds 9–12: Sc around.
Rnd 13: Sc around, dec 8 sc evenly spaced—32 sc. To dec, (insert hook in next st) twice, yo and pull through 3 lps on hook.
Rnd 14: Sc around.
Rnd 15: Sc around, dec 8 sc evenly spaced—24 sc.
Rnds 16 and 17: Sc around. Fill with potpourri. Continue to fill as you crochet.
Rnds 18 and 19: Sc around, dec 8 sc evenly spaced each rnd—8 sc.
Rnd 20: Sc around, dec 4 sc evenly spaced. Cut yarn, leaving an end. Thread end in tapestry needle and pull through remaining 4 sc. Pull tightly and fasten securely.
FINISHING: Scattered Buds: Work French knots randomly spaced on ball for buds, using 12 strands A or B floss and wrapping thread three times around needle (see Embroidery Stitch Details,

page 78). Using 6 strands D floss, embroider one lazy daisy loop horizontally on each side of each bud as shown in color photograph.

Cluster Buds: Work three clusters of 15–25 French knots each on ball, using 12 strands A, B, or C floss for each knot and wrapping thread three times around needle. Using 6 strands D floss, embroider lazy daisy loops around clusters, as shown in color photograph. Using 12 strands floss in needle, work additional clusters, randomly spaced, of 3 French knots each—2 knots in A, B, or C and remaining knot each cluster in D.

Rosettes (make three each E and F): With smaller hook and 6 strands floss, ch 5. Sl st in first ch to form ring.

Rnd 1: * Ch 3, sl st in ring, ch 4, sl st in ring, repeat from * 9 times. End off.

Sew rosettes, alternating colors, evenly spaced around rnd 11 of sachet. With 6 strands G, embroider a row of chain stitch over and under rosettes. With H, embroider another row of chain stitch.

With 12 strands floss, embroider E and F French knots randomly along chain stitches.

Sew beads randomly around ball.

Tassel: With pearl cotton, wrap a 3½″ piece of cardboard 40 times; cut one end. Cut a 6″ strand; set aside. Beg 3″ from ends, wrap center of tassel tightly 30 times, without overlapping; do not cut thread. Fold tassel in half around 6″ strand that was set aside, and wrap entire thickness 5 times. Cut thread. Sew end to bottom of sachet, pull down through center of tassel, over one thread of wrap, and cut this end even while trimming tassel.

Hanger: Fold ribbon in half. Sew ends to top of sachet.

HANGER COVERS

SIZE: Each cover, 17″ long.
MATERIALS (for each hanger): Pearl cotton size 5, five 15-meter (16.4-yard) skeins lavender, blue, or yellow. Crochet hook size 2/C (2.75 mm) or size required to obtain gauge. Wooden hanger, 17″ long. Fiberfill. Satin ribbon ¼″ wide, 6″. White craft glue.
GAUGE: 26 hdc = 4″.
COVER: Ch 106.
Row 1: Hdc in 2nd ch from hook and in each ch across—105 hdc. Ch 2, turn.
Row 2: Hdc in each hdc across. Ch 2, turn each row. Repeat row 2 until piece measures 2″ from beg.
Hook Opening: Hdc in 51 hdc, ch 3, sk 3 hdc, hdc in remaining 51 hdc.
Next Row: Hdc across, working 3 hdc in ch-3 sp. Work even until piece measures 2″ from hook opening. End off.

FINISHING: Fold cover in half lengthwise, wrong side out. Sl st short edges tog. Turn cover right side out; insert hanger. Stuff lightly with fiberfill.

Join thread at bottom corner. Working through both thicknesses, work 100 sc evenly spaced along lower edge.

Lavender Edging: Row 1: * Ch 5, sk 3 sc, sc in next sc, repeat from * across. Turn each row.
Rows 2 and 3: * Ch 5, (sc, ch 3, sc) in 3rd ch of ch-5 sp, repeat from * across. End off.
Blue Edging: Row 1: Ch 1, sc in each sc across, inc 1 sc—101 sc. Ch 7, turn each row.
Row 2: Dc in 6th sc, * ch 4, sk 4 sc, dc in next sc, repeat from * across.
Row 3: * Holding back last lp of each dtr, work 3 dtr in next dc, yo and pull through 4 lps on hook—3-dtr cluster made; ch 4, 3-dtr cluster in same dc, repeat from * across. End off.
Yellow Edging: Row 1: Sc in each sc across, dec 1 sc—99 sc. Ch 4, turn.
Row 2: Dc in 3rd sc, * ch 1, sk 1 sc, dc in next sc, repeat from * across. Ch 1, turn.
Row 3: Sc in each dc and ch-1 sp across, 2 sc in turning ch-4 sp—100 sc. Ch 7, turn.
Row 4: Sl st in 4th sc, * ch 7, sk 3 sc, sl st in next sc, repeat from * across. Turn.
Row 5: In each ch-7 lp, work 3 sc, (yo and pull up a lp) 7 times, yo and pull through 14 lps, yo and pull through remaining 2 lps, work 3 sc. End off.
Hook Cover: Beg at bottom of hook, sc around hook until hook is covered. End off. Pull back worked sc's from tip of hook; spread glue around tip. Push sc's over glue. Let dry. Tie ribbon in bow around base of hook.

FILET CROCHET COLLAR

SIZE: Fits child.
MATERIALS: Crochet cotton size 10, two 50-gram (1.75-oz.) balls white. Steel crochet hook No. 5 or size required to obtain gauge. Satin ribbon ⅜″ wide, ½ yard.
GAUGE: 4 spaces (sps) or blocks (bls) = 1″; 5 rows = 1″.
Collar: Ch 136.
Row 1: Dc in 4th ch from hook and in each ch across—133 dc. Ch 3 (counts as 1 dc), turn each row.
Row 2: Sk first dc, dc in each dc across, dc in turning ch.
Row 3: Sk first dc, dc in next 6 dc, (ch 2, sk 2 dc, dc in next dc) 40 times, dc in next 5 dc, dc in turning ch.
Row 4: 3 dc in first dc—1 bl inc; dc in 3 dc, ch 2, sk 2 dc, dc in next dc, (ch 2, dc in next dc) 29 times, 2 dc in ch-2 sp, dc in next dc, (ch 2, dc in next dc) 10

times, ch 2, sk 2 dc, dc in 3 dc, 4 dc in turning ch—1 bl inc. Continue to follow chart, inc as indicated through row 28.

Row 29: 3 dc in first dc, dc in 3 dc, ch 2, sk 2 dc, dc in next dc, (ch 2, dc in next dc) 4 times, 2 dc in ch-2 sp, dc in next dc, ch 2, sk 2 dc, dc in next dc, (ch 2, dc in next dc) 12 times, (dc in next dc, 2 dc in ch-2 sp) twice, dc in 3 dc, (yo, insert hook in next dc, yo and pull through 2 lps on hook) 3 times—1 bl dec; ch 1, turn, sl st in 3 dc, ch 3.

Row 30: Dec 1 bl as established. Continue to follow chart, inc and dec as indicated, for left half of back collar. Work to top of chart. End off.

Right Back Collar: Skip next 17 dc on last long row, join thread, dec 1 bl, finish row. Work to chart top. Do not end off.

Edging: From right side, in corner of collar, work (dc, ch 3, sl st in top of dc just made—picot) 10 times, working along edge of collar, into sts at end of rows, * sk next 2 rows, sc in end of next row, sk next 2 rows, in end of next row, work (dc, picot) 6 times, repeat from * to lower front edge, work corner same as before, working along lower edge, work into every 6th dc from foundation row. Continue as established along entire collar edge to neck edge.

Neck Edging: (Ch 4, sc in end of next row) around edge.

FINISHING: Block collar. Sew 9″ lengths of satin ribbon to inside back neck edge.

FILET CROCHET COLLAR CHART

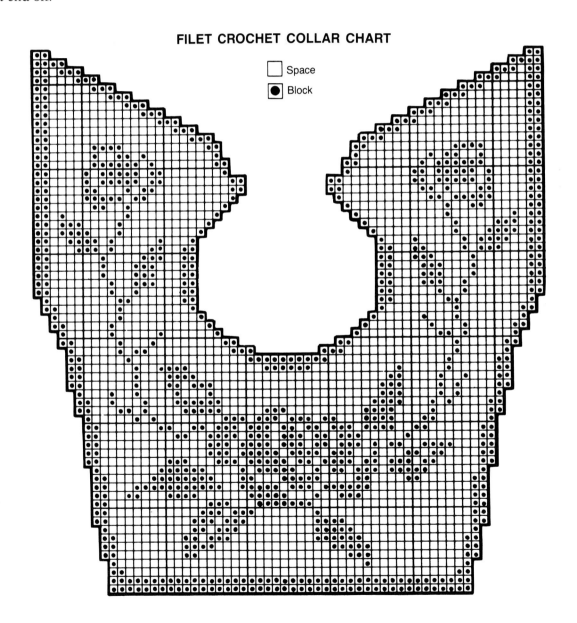

☐ Space
⬤ Block

Take Time to Relax

Cozy and comfortable is how every member of the family will feel using these practical crocheted accessories. Great for the TV room, bedroom, or other informal settings, the afghan, rug, pillows, and ottoman all say, "Take it easy."

PILLOWS

SIZE: 16″ × 16″.
MATERIALS: Worsted weight cotton yarn, 50-gram (1.75-oz.) skeins (see each pillow for quantity and color). Crochet hook size 6/G (4.25 mm) or size required to obtain gauge. Two pieces fabric 16½″ square for each pillow backing. Pillow form 15″ square. Matching sewing thread. Sewing needle. Tapestry needle.
GAUGE: 16 sts = 4″; 17 rows = 4″.
Notes: To change colors insert hook in next st, yo and pull through, yo with new color and pull through 2 lps on hook. When more than one color is used in a single row, work over unused strand with each sc. Follow chart from right to left on right-side rows, from left to right on wrong-side rows.

CHECKED PILLOW

MATERIALS: Two skeins each green (A) and off-white (B).
PILLOW: With A, ch 61.
Row 1: With A, sc in 2nd ch from hook and in next 3 ch, changing to B in 3rd sc (see Notes), * with B, sc in next 4 ch, changing to A in 4th sc, with A, sc in next 4 sc, changing to B in 4th sc, repeat from * across. Ch 1, turn each row.
Rows 2–4: With A, sk first sc, sc in next 3 sc, changing to B in last sc, * with B, sc in 4 sc, changing to A in last sc, with A, sc in 4 sc, changing to B in last sc, repeat from * across, working last sc in ch-1.
Rows 5–8: Work in established pat, beg pat with B and changing to A.
Row 9: Repeat row 2. Repeat rows 1–9 6 times, rows 2–4 once.
Edging: From right side, with A, work 2 rows sc

around, working 2 sc in each corner, sl st in first sc. End off.

GOOSE PILLOW

MATERIALS: Two skeins blue (A), one skein off-white (B), small amounts yellow (C).
PILLOW: With A, ch 57.
Row 1: Sc in 2nd ch from hook and in each ch across—56 sc. Ch 1, turn each row.
Rows 2–30: Sk first sc, sc in 2nd sc and each sc across. Sc in ch-1.
Rows 31 and 32: With B, sk first sc, sc in next sc, changing to A in this st, * with A, sc in 2 sc, changing to B in 2nd sc, with B, sc in 2 sc, changing to A in 2nd sc, repeat from * across, working last sc in ch-1.
Rows 33 and 34: Work same as rows 31 and 32, beg with A and changing to B.
Rows 35 and 36: Work 2 rows A.
Row 37: With B, sk first sc, sc in next sc, * sc in next 6 sc, changing to C in last sc, work 1 sc in C, completing this st with B, with B, sc in next 11 sc, repeat from * twice, following row 1 of chart from right to left (see Notes).
Rows 38–49: Work to top of chart as established.
Rows 50–51: Work 2 rows A.
Rows 52–55: Repeat rows 31–34.
Rows 56–67: Work 12 rows A.
FINISHING: With tapestry needle and C, make 2 long sts over 2 ecru "beak" sts for beak.
Edging: From right side, work 2 rows of sc around pillow, working 2 sc in each corner, join with sl st to first sc. End off.

GOOSE PILLOW CHART

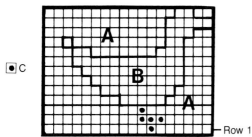

☐ C

— Row 1

STRIPED PILLOW

MATERIALS: Two skeins each pink (A) and blue (B).
PILLOW: With A, ch 57.
Row 1: Sc in 2nd ch from hook and in each ch across—56 sc. Ch 1, turn.
Row 2: Sk first sc, sc in next sc and in each sc across, sc in ch-1.

Row 3: With B, * work 2 sc in next sc, sk next sc, repeat from * across—56 sc.
Rows 4–12: Repeat row 2, working 2 rows A, (1 row B, 1 row A) twice, 1 row B, 2 rows A.
Row 13: Repeat row 3.
Rows 14–18: Work 5 rows A.
Row 19: Repeat row 3.
Rows 20–28: Repeat rows 4–12.
Row 29: Repeat row 3.
Rows 30–40: Work 11 rows A.
Row 41: Repeat row 3.
Rows 42–50: Repeat rows 4–12.
Row 51: Repeat row 3.
Rows 52–56: Work 5 rows A.
Row 57: Repeat row 3.
Rows 58–66: Repeat rows 4–12.
Row 67: Repeat row 3.
Rows 68–69: Work 2 rows A. Do not end off.
Edging: Ch 1, from right side, work 1 row sc around, working 2 sc in each corner. Sl st in first sc, end off.
FINISHING: Pillow Backing: With right sides tog, sew fabric pieces tog along 3 sides, ¾″ from edge. Turn right side out, clipping at corners. Hand-stitch pillow backing to crocheted piece within sc row edging. Insert pillow form and hand-stitch remaining seam.

PLAID AFGHAN

SIZE: 50″ × 58″.
MATERIALS: Bernat Berella 4, seven 100-gram (3.5-oz) skeins green #8821 (A), three skeins each natural #8940 (B) and medium blue #8861 (C); two skeins medium rose #8922 (D). Crochet hook size 10½/K (6.5 mm) or size required to obtain gauge.
GAUGE: 8 sts = 3″.
PAT ST: Row 1: Ch 1, (sc, dc) in first st, * sk next st, (sc, dc) in next st, repeat from * across, end sc in last st.
Row 2: Ch 1, (sc, dc) in first sc, * sk next dc, (sc, dc) in next sc, repeat from * across. Repeat row 2 for pat st.
AFGHAN: With A, ch 150.
Next Row: (Sc, dc) in 2nd ch from hook, * sk next ch, (sc, dc) in next ch, repeat from * across, end sc in last ch—150 sts.
Row 1: Following chart row 1, continue in pat st, working from A to B once, B to C 4 times, C to D once.
Row 2: Following chart row 2, continue in pat st, working from D to C once, from C to B 4 times, from B to A once. Continue to work in pat st, following chart, until piece measures 57½″ from beg. Work 1 row pat st with A. End off.

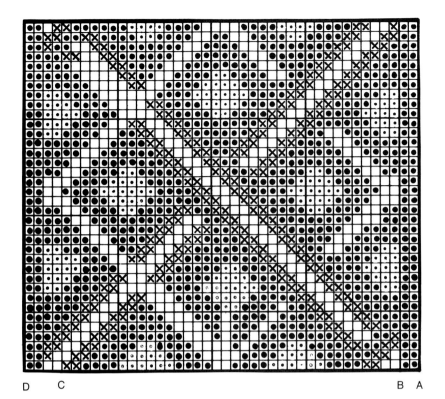

A: ●
B: ☐
C: ☒
D: ⊡

D   C   B   A

GOOSE RUG

SIZE: 23″ × 32″.

MATERIALS: Coats & Clark Red Heart® Heavy Rug Yarn, Art. E. 40, seven 60-yard skeins each blue (A) and white (B); small amount yellow (C). Crochet hook size 8/H (5 mm) or size required to obtain gauge.

GAUGE: 13 sts = 4″; 13 rows = 4″.

Note: To change colors, insert hook in next st, yo and pull through, yo with new color and pull through 2 lps on hook. When more than one color is used in a single row, work over unused strand with each sc.

RUG: With A, ch 77.

Row 1 (right side): Sc in 2nd ch from hook and in each ch across—76 sc. Ch 1, turn each row.

Row 2: Sk first sc, sc in next 3 sc, changing to B in 3rd sc; * with B, sc in next 4 sc, changing to A in 4th sc; with A, sc in next 4 sc, changing to B in 4th sc; repeat from * across, end sc in ch-1.

Rows 3–5: Repeat row 2.

Rows 6–9: Work same as row 2, beg with A, and changing to B.

Rows 10 and 11: Work in A only.

Row 12 (wrong side): With A, sk first sc, sc in next 3 sc, * beg chart row 1 over next 14 sts, following chart from left to right, sc in 4 sc, repeat from * 3 times, working last sc in ch-1.

Rows 13–24: Continue working to top of chart as established.

Rows 25 and 26: Work in A only.

Rows 27–78: Repeat rows 2–9 6 times, rows 2–5 once.

Rows 79 and 80: Work in A only.

Row 81 (right side): With A, sk first sc, sc in next 3 sc, * beg chart over next 14 sts, following chart from left to right, with A, sc in next 4 sc, repeat from * 3 times, working last sc in ch-1.

Rows 82–94: Continue working to top of chart as established. Geese will face in opposite direction from geese at beg of rug.

Rows 95 and 96: Work in A only.

Rows 97–104: Repeat rows 2–5.

Row 105: Work in A only, at end of row, ch 1, do not end off.

EDGING: Working from right side, with a double strand of A, sc in each sc along all 4 sides of rug, working from left to right (corded edge st), working 3 sc in each corner. Sl st in first sc to join. End off.

GOOSE RUG CHART

⊡ C

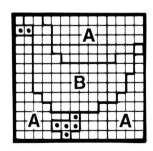

FRINGE: Make 190 9″ lengths of each color by wrapping a 4½″ piece of cardboard and cutting at one end.

Fold 5 strands of A in half; with right side facing, pull center of fringe from front to back through first sc made at lower right edge of rug, forming a lp, pull ends of fringe through lp and tighten. Sk next st, make an A fringe in next st. Continue to make fringes in every other st as established on upper and lower edges of rug.

BASKETS AND BOWS

SIZES: 6″, 8″, and 10″ high. (Instructions that follow are for 6″ basket; for larger baskets increase accordingly.)
MATERIALS: Two bedsheets in floral pattern. Solid color fabric in 3 colors to match floral pattern, ¼ yard each. Crochet hook size Q or size required to obtain gauge.
GAUGE: 4 sc = 4″.
TO PREPARE STRIPS: Cut sheets into strips 1½″ wide. Join strips by overlapping ends slightly and hand-stitching ends tog. Wind into a separate ball for each color, or join strips while working.
6″ BASKET: Beg at center bottom, ch 5. Sl st in first ch to form ring.
Rnd 1: 2 sc in each ch around—10 sc.
Rnd 2: Sc in each sc around—10 sc.
Rnd 3: Repeat rnd 1—20 sc.
Rnd 4: Repeat rnd 2—20 sc.
Rnd 5: Working in back lps only, sc in each sc around—20 sc. Work even on 20 sc until basket is 6″ high, inc 4 sts evenly spaced on last rnd. Sl st in next sc. End off.

Cut solid color fabric into strips 3″ wide. Join ends so strip fits around basket and is long enough to tie a bow. Weave strips around basket 2 rnds below top. Tie ends into a large bow.

OTTOMAN

SIZE: 15″ cube.
MATERIALS: Worsted weight yarn, twenty 50-gram (1.75-oz.) balls blue (A); two balls green (B); one ball each pink (C), yellow (D), and mauve (E). Crochet hooks sizes 5/F and 8/H (3.75 and 5 mm) or size required to obtain gauge. Foam rubber, 15″ cube.
GAUGE: 16 sc = 4″; 16 rows = 4″ (larger hook).
Note: To change colors, insert hook in next st, yo and pull through, yo with new color and pull through 2 lps on hook.
SIDES: (make six): With larger hook and A, ch 61.
Row 1: Sc in 2nd ch from hook and in each ch across—60 sc. Ch 1, turn.
Row 2: Sk first sc, sc tfl (through front lp) of each sc across, sc tfl in turning ch. Ch 1, turn each row. Repeat row 2 until piece measures 15″ from beg. End off.
FINISHING: From right side, sc pieces tog to form cube, using corded edge st (sc worked from left to right) as follows: Join one side square to each edge of a bottom square. Join four sides. Insert foam rubber. Join one edge of top square to each side square.
POCKETS (make two): With larger hook and B, ch 31.
Row 1: Sc in 2nd ch from hook and in each ch across—30 sc. Ch 1, turn each row.
Row 2: Sc in first sc, * sk 1 sc, 2 sc in next sc, repeat from * across.
Rows 3–8: Sc in each sc across. Change to A at end of row 8.
Row 9: With A, repeat row 2.
Rows 10–12: Sc in each sc across. Change to D at end of row 12.
Row 13: With D, repeat row 2.
Rows 14–16: Sc in each sc across. Change to A at end of row 16.
Row 17: With A, repeat row 2.
Rows 18–22: Sc in each sc across. Change to E at end of row 22.
Row 23: With E, repeat row 2.
Rows 24–26: Sc in each sc across. Change to B at end of row 26.
Row 27: With B, repeat row 2.
Rows 28–32: Sc in each sc across. Change to A at end of row 32.
Row 33: With A, repeat row 2.
Rows 34–36: Sc in each sc across. Change to C at end of row 36.
Row 37: With C, repeat row 2.
Rows 38–40: Sc in each sc across. Change to B at end of row 40.
Row 41: With B, repeat row 2.
Rows 42–44: Sc in each sc across. Change to smaller hook at end of row 44.
Row 45: Sc in each sc across. End off.

Sew bottom edge of one pocket to one side of ottoman, 1″ above bottom edge and 3″ from each side edge, gathering pocket to a 9″ width. Turn down top edge of pocket 1″ to right side and tack at side edges. Sew side edges of pocket to ottoman. Sew second pocket to the opposite side of ottoman.

Old Fashion-able Bath

Perk up your ordinary bathroom towels with delightful crocheted motifs and edgings. These country crochet touches can also give a new look to your table and bed linens.

SCALLOPED TOWEL BORDERS

SIZE: 1″ wide.
MATERIALS: Crochet cotton size 30, one ball. Steel crochet hook No. 8 (1.25 mm) or size required to make gauge. Cotton print fabric, ⅛ yard. Satin ribbon ⅛″ wide, to match fabric.
BORDER: Cut a strip of fabric 2″ wide and ½″ longer than width of towel. Turn under ¼″ on all edges; stitch to towel with matching sewing thread.
EDGING: Make a chain 2″ longer than width of towel.
Row 1 (right side): Dc in 8th ch from hook, * ch 2, sk 2 ch, dc in next ch, repeat from * across until edging is same width as towel and there are an uneven number of sps. Ch 1, turn.
Row 2: Sc in first sp, ch 7, sc in same sp, * 2 sc in next sp, sc, ch 7, sc in next sp, repeat from * across. Ch 1, turn.
Row 3: In ch-7 lp work (sc, ch 3) 5 times, * sc in each of next 3 sc, in next lp work (sc, ch 3) 5 times, repeat from * across, end sc in last sc. End off.

Join thread in first sp on opposite side of starting ch at other end of edging. Work rows 2 and 3 of row 1 of edging.
FINISHING: Run ribbon through sps of row 1. Sew edging to center of fabric border along top and bottom edges of row 1. Make a ribbon bow; tack to edging.

TULIP FILET APPLIQUÉ

SIZE: 4″ × 5″.
MATERIALS: Crochet cotton size 50, one ball. Steel crochet hook No. 12 (0.6 mm) or size required to obtain gauge.
GAUGE: 7 sps or bls = 1″; 7 rows = 1″.
APPLIQUÉ: Ch 26.
Row 1: Dc in 8th ch from hook, (ch 2, sk 2 ch, dc in next ch) 6 times, ch 2, tr in same ch as last dc—6 sps, 1 half-sp each end. Ch 7, turn.
Row 2: Dc in tr, (ch 2, dc in next dc) 7 times, ch 2, sk 2 ch of end ch, dc in next ch, ch 2, tr in same ch at last dc—8 sps, 1 half-sp each end. Ch 7, turn.
Row 3: Dc in tr, (ch 2, dc in next dc) 9 times, ch 2, sk 2 ch of end ch, dc in next ch, ch 2, tr in same ch as last dc—10 sps, 1 half-sp each end. Ch 7, turn.

Row 4: Dc in tr, (ch 2, dc in next dc) 11 times, ch 2, sk 2 ch of end ch, dc in next ch, ch 2, tr in same ch as last dc—12 sps, 1 half-sp each end. Ch 7, turn.
Row 5: Dc in tr, (ch 2, dc in next dc) 6 times, (2 dc in next sp, dc in next dc) twice, (ch 2, dc in next dc) 5 times, ch 2, sk 2 ch of end ch, dc, ch 2, tr in next ch—2 bls made at center of design. Ch 7, turn.
Row 6: Dc in tr, (ch 2, dc in next dc) 7 times, dc in next 6 dc—2 bls over 2 bls made—(ch 2, dc in next dc) 6 times, ch 2, sk 2 ch of end ch, dc, ch 2, tr in next ch. Ch 7, turn.

Continue to add 1 half-sp at each end of next 2 rows, following chart for placement of bls. At end of row 8, ch 5, turn.
Row 9: Dc in next dc for first sp, work 6 more sps, 2 bls, 1 sp, 2 bls, 1 sp, 2 bls, 7 sps. Ch 5, turn.
Rows 10–23: Keeping side edges even, follow chart to end of row 23. At end of row 23, ch 4, turn.
Row 24: Sk first dc, dc in next dc, work in pat across to last sp, tr in 3rd ch of turning ch—1 half-sp dec each end. Ch 4, turn.
Row 25: Sk first dc, dc in next dc, work in pat across to last full sp, tr in next dc. Ch 4, turn.
Rows 26–31: Continue to dec 1 sp each end each row, working 1 half-sp each end. At end of row 31, ch 1, do not turn.

TULIP FILET CHART

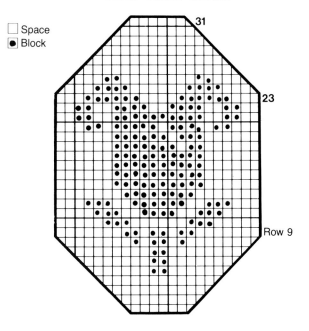

☐ Space
● Block

31

23

Row 9

EDGING: Rnd 1: Working down side of appliqué, * 2 sc in next sp, sc, ch 6, sc in next sp, repeat from * around, end sl st in first sc.

Rnd 2: Sc in 2 sc, * sk next sc, sc in ch-6 lp, (ch 3, sc) 5 times in lp, sk next sc, sc in next 2 sc, repeat from * around, end sl st in first sc. End off. Sew appliqué on towel along filet edge, leaving edging free.

BASKET APPLIQUÉ

SIZE: 5″ wide × 5¾″ high.

MATERIALS: Crochet cotton size 30, one ball. Steel crochet hook No. 10 (0.75 mm) or size required to obtain gauge. Satin ribbon ⅛″ wide, ½ yard.

BASKET: Beg at lower edge, ch 27.

Row 1: Sc in 2nd ch from hook, hdc in next ch, dc in each of next 22 ch, hdc in next ch, sc in last ch. Ch 3, turn.

Row 2: Sk first st, dc in hdc, * ch 1, sk 1 dc, dc in each of next 2 dc, repeat from * across, end ch 1, sk 1 dc, dc in hdc, dc in sc. Ch 3, turn.

Row 3: Dc in first st, ch 1, 2 dc in next dc, (2 dc in next dc, ch 1, 2 dc in next dc) 7 times, 2 dc in next dc, ch 1, 2 dc in top of turning ch—9 shells. Ch 3, turn.

Row 4: Dc, ch 1, 2 dc in ch-1 sp of first shell, (2 dc, ch 1, 2 dc in ch-1 sp of next shell) 8 times. Ch 3, turn.

Rows 5 and 6: Repeat row 4.

Row 7: 2 dc, ch 1, 3 dc in ch-1 sp of first shell, (3 dc, ch 1, 3 dc in ch-1 sp of next shell) 8 times. Ch 3, turn.

Row 8: Repeat row 7.

Row 9: 2 dc, ch 1, 3 dc in ch-1 sp of first shell, (ch 1, 3 dc, ch 1, 3 dc in ch-1 sp of next shell) 8 times. Ch 3, turn.

Row 10: 2 dc, ch 1, 3 dc in ch-1 sp of first shell, (ch 2, 3 dc, ch 1, 3 dc in ch-1 sp of next shell) 8 times. Ch 3, turn.

Rows 11 and 12: Work as for row 10 but ch 3 between shells.

Row 13: 2 dc, ch 3, 3 dc in ch-1 sp of first shell, (ch 3, 3 dc, ch 3, 3 dc in ch-1 sp of next shell) 8 times. Ch 3, turn.

Row 14: (right side): 10 dc in ch-3 sp of each shell across. End off.

From right side, join thread in first st on opposite side of starting ch. Working in each ch across, work sc, hdc, 4 dc, 14 tr, 4 dc, hdc, sc. End off.

HANDLE: Ch 5.

Row 1: 2 tr, ch 2, 3 tr in 5th ch from hook. Turn.

Row 2: Sl st across to ch-2 sp, ch 4, 2 tr, ch 2, 3 tr in ch-2 sp. Turn.

Rows 3–22: Repeat row 2. End off.

FLOWER (make three): Ch 6; sl st in first ch to form ring.

Rnd 1: Ch 6, dc in ring (ch 3, dc in ring) 3 times, ch 3, sl st in 3rd ch of ch-6—5 lps.

Rnd 2: In each lp work sc, hdc, 4 dc, hdc, sc; sl st in first st—5 petals. End off.

FINISHING: Run ribbon through rows 2 and 12 of basket and through center sps of handle. Sew ends of handle to last row of basket between second and third shells from each end. Sew basket to towel. Sew flowers in place.

HEART TOWEL EDGING

MATERIALS: Crochet cotton size 30, one ball. Steel crochet hook No. 8 (1.25 mm). Ribbon ⅛″ wide, ⅝ yard.

EDGING: Make a ch 14″ long.

Row 1: Dc in 8th ch from hook, * ch 2, sk 2 ch, dc in next ch, repeat from * across until edging is about 12″ long. Ch 1, turn. Cut off extra ch.

Row 2: Sc in first sp, ch 7, sc in same sp, * 2 sc in next sp, sc, ch 7, sc in next sp, repeat from * across. Ch 1, turn.

Row 3: In ch-7 lp work (sc, ch 3) 5 times, * sc in each of next 3 sc, in next lp work (sc, ch 3) 5 times, repeat from * across, end sc in last sc. End off.

FINISHING: Weave ribbon through sps of row 1. Form heart shape with edging, pin to towel with ends of edging at center top. Sew edging to towel along both edges of row 1, leaving rows 2 and 3 free. Form a ribbon bow; tack to center top of heart.

TULIP APPLIQUÉ TOWEL EDGINGS

MATERIALS: Crochet cotton size 30, one ball. Steel crochet hook No. 8 (1.25 mm). Ribbon ⅛″ wide.
EDGING: For Hand Towel: Make a ch 12″ long.
Row 1: Dc in 8th ch from hook, * ch 2, sk 2 ch, dc in next ch, repeat from * across until piece fits width of towel and there are odd number of sps. Cut extra ch. Ch 1, turn.

Row 2: Sc, ch 6, sc in first sp, * 2 sc in next sp, sc, ch 6, sc in next sp, repeat from * across. Ch 1, turn.
Row 3: Sc in next lp, (ch 3, sc) 5 times in same lp, * sk next sc, sc in 2 sc, sk next sc, sc in next lp, (ch 3, sc) 5 times in same lp, repeat from * across. End off.

Run ribbon through row 1 of edging. Sew edging to towel along top and bottom edges of row 1. Make ribbon bow, tack to tulip appliqué.
For Larger Towels: Work 2 rows of filet crochet sps, then work rows 2 and 3 as for hand towel. Run ribbon through both rows of filet sps.

Window Enchantment

Sheer curtains are great window enhancers, but why not try crocheted panels instead, for the same elegant effect? Here are two designs to use as full- or part-length curtains or as shutter inserts. (The full-length designs can be adapted for shorter ones.)

SPIDER WEB CURTAINS

SIZE: One panel, 72″ × 40″.
MATERIALS: DMC Brilliant Crochet Cotton, twenty 218-yard balls ecru for one panel. Steel crochet hook No. 6 (1.75 mm) or size required to obtain gauge.
GAUGE: 9 dc = 1″; 4 rows = 1″.
PANEL: Lower Border: Beg at right edge of lower border, ch 34.
Row 1: Dc in 9th ch from hook, and in each ch across—26 dc. Ch 4, sc in 4th ch from hook for ch-4 picot, turn.
Row 2: Dc in each dc across, ch 2, sk 2 ch of end ch, dc in next ch. Ch 5, turn.
Row 3: Sk ch-2 sp, dc in each of next 12 dc, ch 2, sk 2 dc, dc in each of next 12 dc. Ch-4 picot, turn.
Row 4: Dc in 10 dc, ch 3, dc in ch-2 sp, ch 3, sk 2 dc, dc in next 10 dc, ch 2, sk 2 ch of end ch, dc in next ch. Ch 5, turn.
Row 5: Dc in 8 dc, ch 4, sk 2 ch, sc in next ch, sc in dc, sc in next ch, ch 4, sk 2 dc, dc in next 8 dc. Ch-4 picot, turn.
ow 6: Dc in 6 dc, ch 6, sk 3 ch, sc in next ch, sc in 3 sc, sc in next ch, ch 6, sk 2 dc, dc in next 6 dc, ch 2, sk 2 ch of end ch, dc in next ch. Ch 5, turn.
Row 7: Dc in 6 dc, 2 dc in next sp, ch 5, sk 1 sc, sc in next 3 sc, ch 5, 2 dc in next sp, dc in next 6 dc. Ch-4 picot, turn.
Row 8: Dc in 8 dc, 2 dc in next sp, ch 3, sk 1 sc, tr in

next sc, ch 3, 2 dc in next sp, dc in next 8 dc, ch 2, sk 2 ch of end ch, dc in next ch. Ch 5, turn.

Row 9: Dc in 10 dc, 2 dc in next sp, ch 2, 2 dc in next sp, dc in next 10 dc. Ch-4 picot, turn.

Row 10: Dc in 12 dc, 2 dc in ch-2 sp, dc in next 12 dc, ch 2, sk 2 ch of end ch, dc in next ch. Ch 5, turn.

Row 11: Dc in 26 dc across. Ch-4 picot, turn.

Row 12: Ch 1, sk first dc, dc in next dc, (ch 1, sk 1 dc, dc in next dc) 12 times, ch 2, sk 2 ch of end ch, dc in next ch. Ch 5, turn.

Row 13: Dc in next dc, (dc in ch-1 sp, dc in next dc) 12 times, dc in ch-1 sp—26 dc. Ch-4 picot, turn.

Row 14: Dc in each of next 12 dc, ch 2, sk 2 dc, dc in each of next 12 dc, ch 2, sk 2 ch of end ch, dc in next ch. Ch 5, turn.

Row 15: Dc in 10 dc, ch 3, dc in ch-2 sp, ch 3, sk 2 dc, dc in next 10 dc. Ch-4 picot, turn.

Row 16: Dc in 8 dc, ch 4, sk 2 ch, sc in next ch, sc in dc, sc in next ch, ch 4, sk 2 dc, dc in next 8 dc, ch 2, sk 2 ch of end ch, dc in next ch. Ch 5, turn.

Row 17: Dc in 6 dc, ch 6, sk 3 ch, sc in next ch, sc in 3 sc, sc in next ch, ch 6, sk 2 dc, dc in next 6 dc. Ch-4 picot, turn.

Row 18: Dc in 6 dc, 2 dc in next sp, ch 5, sk 1 sc, sc in next 3 sc, ch 5, 2 dc in next sp, dc in next 6 dc, ch 2, sk 2 ch of end ch, dc in next ch. Ch 5, turn.

Row 19: Dc in 8 dc, 2 dc in next sp, ch 3, sk 1 sc, tr in next sc, ch 3, 2 dc in next sp, dc in next 8 dc. Ch-4 picot, turn.

Row 20: Dc in 10 dc, 2 dc in next sp, ch 2, 2 dc in next sp, dc in next 10 dc, ch 2, sk 2 ch of end ch, dc in next ch. Ch 5, turn.

Row 21: Dc in 12 dc, 2 dc in ch-2 sp, dc in next 12 dc. Ch-4 picot, turn.

Rows 22–149: Repeat rows 12–21 16 times—17 pats, plus starting pat.

Row 150: Ch 1, sk first dc, dc in next dc, (ch 1, sk 1 dc, dc in next dc) 12 times, ch 2, sk 2 ch of end ch, dc in next ch. Ch 5, turn.

Row 151: Dc in next dc, (dc in ch-1 sp, dc in next dc) 12 times, dc in ch-1 sp—26 dc. Ch-4 picot, turn.

Row 152: Dc in each dc across, ch 2, sk 2 ch of end ch, dc in next ch. Ch 5, turn.

Rows 153–161: Repeat rows 3–11.

Row 162: Sk first dc, sc in next dc, (ch-4 picot, sk 1 dc, sc in next dc) 12 times, ch-4 picot, sk 2 ch of end ch, sc in next ch. End off.

Attach thread at starting end of border at lower edge (picot edge), work picot edge across starting ch to correspond to row 162, end ch-4 picot, sk 2 ch of end ch, sc in next ch. Do not end off.

Pattern: Row 1: Working across filet edge of border, make picot, dc in same ch as last sc, dc in each of next 2 ch, * dc in end of row, dc in next sp, repeat from * 8 times, dc in end of row, 2 dc in next sp, 2 dc in end of row—26 dc across end pat—** (ch 2, dc in end of next row) 9 times, 2 dc in next sp, dc in next dc, repeat from ** 12 times, (ch 2, dc in next dc) 9 times, work 26 dc across end pat. Make picot, turn.

Row 2: Dc in each of 12 dc, ch 2, sk 2 dc, dc in next 12 dc, (ch 2, dc in next dc) 8 times, * 2 dc in next sp, dc in next dc, ch 3, sk 2 dc, dc in next dc, 2 dc in next sp, dc in next dc, (ch 2, dc in next dc) 7 times, repeat from * 11 times, 2 dc in next sp, dc in next dc, ch 3, sk 2 dc, dc in next dc, 2 dc in next sp, dc in next dc, (ch 2, dc in next dc) 8 times, dc in 11 dc, ch 2, sk 2 dc, dc in 12 dc. Make picot, turn.

Row 3: Dc in each of 10 dc, ch 3, dc in ch-2 sp, ch 3, sk 2 dc, dc in next 10 dc, (ch 2, dc in next dc) 7 times, * 2 dc in next sp, dc in next dc, ch 3, dc in next sp, ch 3, sk 3 dc, dc in next dc, 2 dc in next sp, dc in next dc, (ch 2, dc in next dc) 5 times, repeat from * 11 times, 2 dc in next sp, dc in next dc, ch 3, dc in next sp, ch 3, sk 3 dc, dc in next dc, 2 dc in next sp, dc in next dc, (ch 2, dc in next dc) 7 times, dc in next 9 dc, ch 3, dc in ch-2 sp, ch 3, sk 2 dc, dc in next 10 dc. Make picot, turn.

Row 4: Dc in each of 8 dc, ch 4, sk 2 ch, sc in next ch, sc in dc, sc in next ch, ch 4, sk 2 dc, dc in next 8 dc, (ch 2, dc in next dc) 6 times, * 2 dc in next sp, dc in next dc, ch 4, sk 2 ch, sc in next ch, sc in dc, sc in next ch, ch 4, sk 3 dc, dc in next dc, 2 dc in next sp, dc in next dc, (ch 2, dc in next dc) 3 times, repeat from * 11 times, 2 dc in next sp, dc in next dc, ch 4, sk 2 ch, sc in next ch, sc in dc, sc in next ch, ch 4, sk 3 dc, dc in next dc, 2 dc in next sp, dc in next dc, (ch 2, dc in next dc) 6 times, dc in next 7 dc, ch 4, sk 2 ch, sc in next ch, sc in dc, sc in next ch, ch 4, sk 2 dc, dc in 8 dc. Make picot, turn.

Row 5: Dc in each of 6 dc, ch 6, sk 3 ch, sc in next ch, sc in 3 sc, sc in next ch, ch 6, sk 2 dc, dc in next 6 dc, (ch 2, dc in next dc) 5 times, * 2 dc in next sp, dc in next dc, ch 6, sk 3 ch of ch-4, sc in next ch, sc in 3 sc, sc in next ch, ch 6, sk 3 dc, dc in next dc, 2 dc in next sp, dc in next dc, ch 2, dc in next dc, repeat from * 11 times, 2 dc in next sp, dc in next dc, ch 6, sk 3 ch of ch-4, sc in next ch, sc in 3 sc, sc in next ch, ch 6, sk 3 dc, dc in next dc, 2 dc in next sp, dc in next dc, (ch 2, dc in next dc) 5 times, dc in next 5 dc, ch 6, sk 3 ch, sc in next ch, sc in 3 sc, sc in next ch, ch 6, sk 2 dc, dc in 6 dc. Make picot, turn.

Row 6: Dc in each of 6 dc, 2 dc in next sp, ch 5, sk 1 sc, sc in next 3 sc, ch 5, 2 dc in next sp, dc in next 6 dc, (ch 2, dc in next dc) 5 times, ch 2, sk 2 dc, dc in next dc, * 3 dc in next sp, ch 5, sk 1 sc, sc in next 3 sc, ch 5, 3 dc in next sp, dc in next dc, ch 3, dc in ch-2 sp, ch 3, sk 3 dc, dc in next dc, repeat from * 11 times, 3 dc in next sp, ch 5, sk 1 sc, sc in next 3 sc, ch 5, 3 dc in next sp, dc in next dc, ch 2, sk 2 dc, dc in next dc, (ch 2, dc in next dc) 5 times, dc in next 5 dc,

2 dc in next sp, ch 5, sk 1 sc, sc in next 3 sc, ch 5, 2 dc in next sp, dc in 6 dc. Make picot, turn.

Row 7: Dc in each of 8 dc, 2 dc in next sp, ch 3, sk 1 sc, tr in next sc, ch 3, 2 dc in next sp, dc in 8 dc, (ch 2, dc in next dc) 6 times, ch 2, sk 2 dc, dc in next dc, * 3 dc in next sp, ch 3, sk 1 sc, tr in next sc, ch 3, 3 dc in next sp, dc in next dc, ch 4, sk 2 ch, sc in next ch, sc in dc, sc in next ch, ch 4, sk 3 dc, dc in next dc, repeat from * 11 times, 3 dc in next sp, ch 3, sk 1 sc, tr in next sc, ch 3, 3 dc in next sp, dc in next dc, ch 2, sk 2 dc, dc in next dc, (ch 2, dc in next dc) 6 times, dc in next 7 dc, 2 dc in next sp, ch 3, sk 1 sc, tr in next sc, ch 3, 2 dc in next sp, dc in 8 dc. Make picot, turn.

Row 8: Dc in each of 10 dc, 2 dc in next sp, ch 2, 2 dc in next sp, dc in 10 dc, (ch 2, dc in next dc) 7 times, ch 2, sk 2 dc, dc in next dc. * 3 dc in next sp, ch 2, 3 dc in next sp, dc in next dc, ch 6, sk 3 ch of ch-4, sc in next ch, sc in 3 sc, sc in next ch, ch 6, sk 3 dc, dc in next dc, repeat from * 11 times, 3 dc in next sp, ch 2, 3 dc in next sp, dc in next dc, ch 2, sk 2 dc, dc in next dc, (ch 2, dc in next dc) 7 times, dc in next 9 dc, 2 dc in next sp, ch 2, 2 dc in next sp, dc in 10 dc. Make picot, turn.

Row 9: Dc in each of 10 dc, ch 3, dc in ch-2 sp, ch 3, sk 2 dc, dc in next 10 dc, (ch 2, dc in next dc) 7 times, 2 dc in next sp, dc in next dc, * ch 3, dc in next sp, ch 3, sk 3 dc, dc in next dc, 3 dc in next sp, ch 5, sk 1 sc, sc in 3 sc, ch 5, 3 dc in next sp, dc in next dc, repeat from * 11 times, ch 3, dc in next sp, ch 3, sk 3 dc, dc in next dc, 2 dc in next sp, dc in next dc, (ch 2, dc in next dc) 7 times, dc in next 9 dc, ch 3, dc in ch-2 sp, ch 3, sk 2 dc, dc in 10 dc. Make picot, turn.

Row 10: Dc in each of 8 dc, ch 4, sk 2 ch, sc in next ch, sc in dc, sc in next ch, ch 4, sk 2 dc, dc in next 8 dc, (ch 2, dc in next dc) 6 times, 2 dc in next sp, dc in next dc, * ch 4, sk 2 ch, sc in next ch, sc in dc, sc in next ch, ch 4, sk 3 dc, dc in next dc, 3 dc in next sp, ch 3, sk 1 sc, tr in next sc, ch 3, 3 dc in next sp, dc in next dc, repeat from * 11 times, ch 4, sk 2 ch, sc in next ch, sc in dc, sc in next ch, ch 4, sk 3 dc, dc in next dc, 2 dc in next sp, dc in next dc, (ch 2, dc in next dc) 6 times, dc in next 7 dc, ch 4, sk 2 ch, sc in next ch, sc in dc, sc in next ch, ch 4, sk 2 dc, dc in 8 dc. Make picot, turn.

Row 11: Dc in each of 6 dc, ch 6, sk 3 ch, sc in next ch, sc in 3 sc, sc in next ch, ch 6, sk 2 dc, dc in next 6 dc, (ch 2, dc in next dc) 5 times, 2 dc in next sp, dc in next dc, * ch 6, sk 3 ch of ch-4, sc in next ch, sc in 3 sc, sc in next ch, ch 6, sk 3 dc, dc in next dc, 3 dc in next sp, ch 3, 3 dc in next sp, dc in next dc, repeat from * 11 times, ch 6, sk 3 ch of ch-4, sc in next ch, sc in 3 sc, sc in next ch, ch 6, sk 3 dc, dc in next dc, 2

dc in next sp, dc in next dc, (ch 2, dc in next dc) 5 times, dc in next 5 dc, ch 6, sk 3 ch, sc in next ch, sc in 3 sc, sc in next ch, ch 6, sk 2 dc, dc in 6 dc. Make picot, turn.

Repeat rows 6–11 until panel is 70″ long, or 2″ less than desired finished length, end row 11.

SLOTS FOR CURTAIN ROD: First Opening: Row 1: Dc in 6 dc, ch 3, turn.

Row 2: Sk first dc, dc in 5 dc. Make picot, turn.

Row 3: Dc in 5 dc, dc in top of turning ch. Ch 3, turn.

Rows 4–7: Repeat rows 2 and 3 twice, end row 7, ch 2, do not turn.

Working down edge of slot, sl st in top of row 6, (ch 2, sl st in next row) 6 times, sl st in ch-6 sp, ch 3 for 1 dc, dc in sp, ch 5, sk 1 sc, sc in next 3 sc, ch 5, 2 dc in next sp, dc in next 6 dc, (ch 2, dc in next dc) 4 times. Ch 5, turn.

2nd Opening: Row 1: Dc in next dc, (ch 2, dc in next dc) 3 times. Continue in established pat between first and 2nd openings for 7 rows, end row 6 of pat. Working down edge of slot, (ch 2, sl st in top of next row) 7 times.

3rd Opening: Row 1: Ch 2, dc in next dc, ch 2, sk 2 dc, dc in next dc, 3 dc in next sp, ch 5, sk 1 sc, sc in next 3 sc, ch 5, 3 dc in next sp, dc in next dc, ch 2, sk 2 dc, dc in next dc. Ch 5 turn.

Row 2: Dc in next dc, ch 2, sk 2 dc, dc in next dc, 3 dc in next sp, ch 3, tr in center sc of 3 sc, ch 3, 3 dc in next sp, dc in next dc, ch 2, sk 2 dc, dc in next dc, ch 2, dc in next dc. Ch 5, turn.

Row 3: Dc in next dc, ch 2, dc in next dc, ch 2, sk 2 dc, dc in next dc, 3 dc in next sp, ch 2, 3 dc in next sp, dc in next dc, ch 2, sk 2 dc, dc in next dc, ch 2, dc in next dc, ch 2, sk 2 ch of turning ch, dc in 3rd ch. Ch 5, turn.

Row 4: Dc in next dc, (ch 2, dc in next dc) twice, ch 2, sk 2 dc, dc in next dc, 2 dc in sp, dc in next dc, ch 2, sk 2 dc, dc in next dc, (ch 2, dc in next dc) twice, ch 2, sk 2 ch of turning ch, dc in 3rd ch. Ch 5, turn.

Rows 5–7: Work 9 sps across. At end of row 7, working down edge of slot, (ch 2, sl st in top of next row) 7 times.

Repeat 3rd opening 12 times, then work last 2 slots to correspond to first 2 slots.

Joining Openings: Row 1: Sc in 6 dc, sc in 4 dc, 4 sc in next sp, sc in 3 sc, 4 sc in next sp, sc in 8 dc, 2 sc in each of 4 sps, * sc in sp at edge of slot, 2 sc in each of next 9 sps, repeat from * 12 times, sc in sp at edge of slot, 2 sc in each of next 4 sps, sc in 8 dc, 4 sc in next sp, sc in 3 sc, 4 sc in next sp, sc in each dc to end. Make picot, turn.

Row 2: Sk first sc, sc in next sc, * make picot, sk next sc, sc in next sc, repeat from * across. End off.

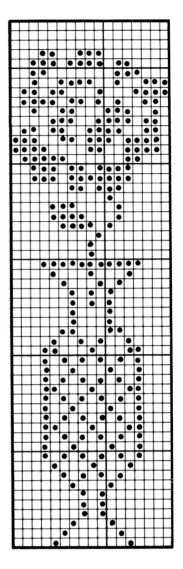

□ Space
● Block

FILET CROCHET SHUTTERS

SIZE: 6″ × 15″.

MATERIALS: Pearl cotton #5, nine balls for four panels. Steel crochet hook No. 5 or size required to obtain gauge. Lining fabric, ½ yard. Matching sewing thread.

GAUGE: 3 sps or bls = 1″; 15 rows = 4″.

PANEL: Beg at lower edge, ch 57.

Row 1: Sc in 2nd ch from hook and in each ch—56 sc. Ch 1, turn.

Row 2: Sc in each sc across. Ch 2, turn.

Row 3: Sk first sc, dc in each of next 2 sc, (ch 2, sk 2 sc, dc in next sc) 4 times (4 sps made), dc in each of next 3 sc (1 bl made), (ch 2, sk 2 sc, dc in next sc) 7 times, (7 sps made), dc in each of next 3 sc (1 bl made), (ch 2, sk 2 sc, dc in next sc) 4 times (4 sps made), dc in last 2 sc. Ch 2, turn.

Row 4: Sk first dc, dc in next 2 dc, (ch 2, dc in next dc) 4 times, ch 2, sk 2 dc, dc in next dc (sp over bl made), dc in each of next 2 ch, dc in next dc (bl over sp made), (ch 2, dc in next dc) 5 times, dc in each of next 2 ch, dc in next dc, ch 2, sk 2 dc, dc in next dc, (ch 2, dc in next dc) 4 times, dc in last 2 dc. Ch 2, turn.

Keeping 3 dc at each side edge, follow chart from 3rd row of chart to top. Ch 1, turn.

Next row: Sc in each dc and ch across. Ch 1, turn.

Last row: Sc in each sc across. End off.

FINISHING: Cut a 7½″ × 17″ piece of lining fabric for each panel. Turn under ¾″ at each side edge of lining; turn under raw edge; machine-stitch hem in place. Turn under 1″ at each end and stitch a casing for rods to go through. Tack a crocheted panel to each lining piece.

KITCHEN AND DINING ACCENTS

Whether you are a full-time homemaker or someone who puts in minimal time in the kitchen, you want to enjoy preparing and eating your meals amid pleasant surroundings. Crochet is perfect for adding decorative and practical touches to the kitchen and dining areas of your home, as well as for making gift accessories to give to others.

Lacy Medallion Table Cover

Here's the perfect solution if your table changes size as leaves are added or subtracted. You can make this cloth in any size, and its two different medallion patterns will always be attractive. The visual effect of the cloth can also be varied by changing the lining fabric beneath it.

SIZE: 44″ × 60″.

MATERIALS: J. & P. Coats Knit-Cro-Sheen, Art. A. 64, twenty-five 225-yd. balls white. Steel crochet hook No. 4 (2 mm) or size required to obtain gauge.

GAUGE: Medallion is 4″ from point to opposite point.

TABLECLOTH: FIRST MOTIF: Ch 8. Sl st in first ch to form ring.

Rnd 1: Ch 3 (counts as first dc), 23 dc in ring. Sl st in top of ch 3.

Rnd 2: Ch 5 (counts as 1 dc, ch 2), sk 1 dc, dc in next dc, * ch 2, sk 1 dc, dc in next dc, repeat from * around, end ch 2, sk last dc, sl st in 3rd ch of ch-5—12 ch-2 sps.

Rnd 3: Ch 3, * 3 dc in next sp, dc in next dc, repeat from * around, end 3 dc in last sp, sl st in top of ch-3—48 dc.

Rnd 4: Ch 7 (counts as 1 dc, ch 4), sk 3 dc, dc in next dc, * ch 4, sk 3 dc, dc in next dc, repeat from * around, end ch 4, sk last 3 dc, sl st in 3rd ch of ch-7—12 ch-4 sps.

Rnd 5: Ch 3, * (4 dc in next sp, dc in next dc) twice, 5 dc in next sp, dc in next dc, repeat from * around, end 5 dc in last sp, sl st in top of ch-3—64 dc.

Rnd 6: Ch 1, sc in same st as sl st, (ch 4, sk 3 dc, tr, ch 3, tr in next dc, ch 4, sk 3 dc, sc in next dc) 8 times, end last repeat sl st in first sc.

Rnd 7: Ch 1, sc in same place as sl st, * in next ch-4 sp work hdc, 3 dc; dc in next tr; in ch-3 sp work 2 dc, ch 1, 2 dc; dc in next tr; in next ch-4 sp work 3 dc, hdc; sc in next sc; repeat from * around, end last repeat sl st in first sc—8 points. End off.

SECOND MOTIF: Work as for first motif until 2 points have been completed; (in next ch-4 sp work hdc, 3 dc; dc in tr; in ch-3 sp work 2 dc, sl st in ch-1 sp of first motif, ch 1, 2 dc in ch-3 sp of second motif, dc in tr; 3 dc, hdc in next ch-4 sp, sc in sc) twice; complete second motif as for first motif.

Make first row of 15 motifs, joining each motif to 2 points opposite last 2 points joined. Make 11 rows of 15 motifs, joining 2 points on side of each motif to corresponding 2 points on preceding row of motifs.

FILL-IN MOTIF: Ch 8. Sl st in first ch to form ring.

Rnd 1: Ch 3, 15 dc in ring, sl st in top of ch-3.

Rnd 2: Ch 5, dc in next dc, (ch 2, dc in next dc) 14 times, ch 2, sl st in 3rd ch of ch-5—16 ch-2 sps.

Rnd 3: * Ch 3, insert hook in joining of 2 points, draw up a lp, sl st in last ch of ch-3, ch 3, sc in next dc, 2 sc in next ch-2 sp, sc in next dc, ch 3, insert hook in sp between 2 points, draw up a lp, sl st in last ch of ch-3; ch 3, sc in next dc, 2 sc in next ch-2 sp, sc in next dc, repeat from * 3 times, end 2 sc in last ch-2 sp, sl st in base of ch-3. End off.

FINISHING: Starch lightly and block to measurements.

Breakfast Table Ensemble

This is a crocheted table ensemble that's a real eye opener. Place mats, napkin rings, hot pad, and napkin holder can be stenciled to coordinate with your china or stoneware patterns. What a lovely way to start the day.

SIZE: Place mat, 17″ × 13″. Napkin ring, 2¼″. Hot mat, 11″ diameter. Napkin holder, 6¼″ high × 6¾″ wide.

MATERIALS: Caron Wintuk, 100-gram (3.5-oz.) skeins, two skeins each blue #351 (A), natural #336 (B); these amounts are enough for two place mats, two napkin rings, one hot mat and one napkin holder; one more skein of each color will make two more place mats and napkin rings. Crochet hook size F (3.75 mm) or size required to obtain gauge. Plaid Stencil Paints: one jar each China Blue, Candy Apple Red, Cameo Green. One sheet stencil film. White glue. Plastic napkin holder, 7½″ × 2¼″ × 6″. Cardboard, two 6″ squares.

GAUGE: 4 sc = 1″; 4 rows = 1″.

PLACE MAT

With A, ch 47.

Row 1: Sc in 2nd ch from hook and in each ch across—46 sc. Ch 1, turn.

Row 2: Sc in each sc across. Ch 1, turn. Repeat row 2 31 times. Work 1 rnd of sc around piece, working 1 sc in each row and st, 3 sc in each corner. End off.

Border: Rnd 1: With B, make lp on hook, sc in any sc, sc in each sc around, 3 sc in each corner st, sl st in first sc.

Rnd 2: Ch 1, sc in first sc, sc in each sc around, 3 sc in each corner st, sl st in first sc.

Rnds 3–7: Repeat rnd 2. Change to A at end of rnd 7.

Rnds 8 and 10: With A, repeat rnd 2.
Rnd 9: With B, repeat rnd 2.

NAPKIN RING

With B, ch 24, sl st in first ch to form ring.
Rnd 1: Ch 1, sc in each ch around—24 sc. Sl st in first sc.
Rnds 2–7: Ch 1, sc in each sc around. Sl st in first sc. Change to A, work 1 rnd of sc. End off. Join A on opposite side of napkin ring, work 1 rnd sc in foundation ch. End off.

HOT MAT

Beg at center with A, ch 2.
Rnd 1: 8 sc in 2nd ch from hook. Sl st in first sc.
Rnd 2: Ch 1, 2 sc in each sc around—16 sc. Sl st in first sc.
Rnd 3: Ch 1, sc in first sc, 2 sc in next sc, (sc in next sc, 2 sc in next sc) 7 times—24 sc. Sl st in first sc.
Rnd 4: Ch 1, sc in first sc and in next sc, 2 sc in next sc, (sc in 2 sc, 2 sc in next sc) 7 times—32 sc. Sl st in first sc.
Note: Begin each rnd with ch 1, sc in first sc and end each rnd with sl st in first sc.

Rnd 5: (Sc in 3 sc, 2 sc in next sc) 8 times—40 sc.
Rnd 6: Sc in each sc around—40 sc.
Rnd 7: (Sc in 4 sc, 2 sc in next sc) 8 times—48 sc.
Rnd 8: (Sc in 5 sc, 2 sc in next sc) 8 times—56 sc.
Rnd 9: (Sc in 6 sc, 2 sc in next sc) 8 times—64 sc.
Rnd 10: (Sc in 7 sc, 2 sc in next sc) 8 times—72 sc.
Rnd 11: Sc in each sc around—72 sc.
Rnd 12: (Sc in 8 sc, 2 sc in next sc) 8 times—80 sc.
Rnd 13: (Sc in 9 sc, 2 sc in next sc) 8 times—88 sc. Cut A; join B.
Rnd 14: With B, (sc in 10 sc, 2 sc in next sc) 8 times—96 sc.
Rnd 15: (Sc in 11 sc, 2 sc in next sc) 8 times—104 sc.
Rnd 16: Sc in each sc around—104 sc.
Rnd 17: (Sc in 12 sc, 2 sc in next sc) 8 times—112 sc.
Rnd 18: (Sc in 13 sc, 2 sc in next sc) 8 times—120 sc.
Rnd 19: (Sc in 14 sc, 2 sc in next sc) 8 times—128 sc.
Rnd 20: Sc in each sc around—128 sc.
Rnd 21: (Sc in 15 sc, 2 sc in next sc) 8 times—136 sc. End off B; join A.
Rnd 22: With A, (sc in 16 sc, 2 sc in next sc) 8 times—144 sc. End off.

NAPKIN HOLDER

SQUARE: (make two A, two B): Ch 23.
Row 1: Sc in 2nd ch from hook and in each ch—22 sc. Ch 1, turn.

Row 2: Sc in each sc across. Ch 1, turn. Repeat row 2 21 times. Work 1 rnd of sc on all 4 sides of square, working 1 sc in each st and row, 3 sc in each corner. End off.

STRIP: With A, make a ch to measure width of inside of napkin holder, plus 1 ch. Work even in sc until strip is long enough to cover bottom of napkin holder. End off.

FINISHING: Stencil B squares before assembling pieces. Glue strip to inside bottom of napkin holder. Beg at lower right corner of B square, with A, sc across lower edge, work 3 sc in corner. Holding A square in back of B square, wrong sides tog, sc B square to A square along side and top edges, leaving bottom edges open. Join other two squares in same way.

Slip a 6″ square of cardboard inside each joined square, then slip squares over sides of napkin holder. With A in tapestry needle, join lower edges of squares on either side of base of napkin holder, carrying yarn underneath holder.

Stenciling

EQUIPMENT: See Materials, page 30. Masking tape. Craft knife. Stencil brushes, at least one for each color paint. Small jars with lids. Saucer for palette. Paper towels. Old newspapers. Brown paper. Iron. Press cloth.

DIRECTIONS: Read all directions below and those with stencil film, and test paints on a sample swatch of crochet before beginning work.

Cover work surface with newspapers, then brown paper; tape in place. Tape crocheted block on top with edges square. Center stencil motif on crocheted block; tape or press in place. Do not move stencil while working, or paint will smear.

Stencil each color on design, following illustration for colors. When working on one area of sten-

BORDER STENCIL

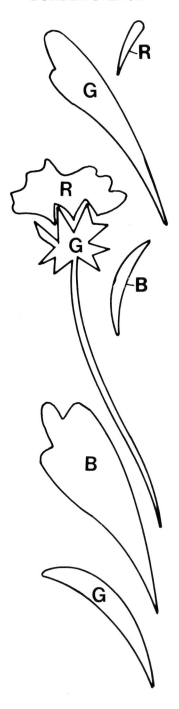

NAPKIN HOLDER STENCIL

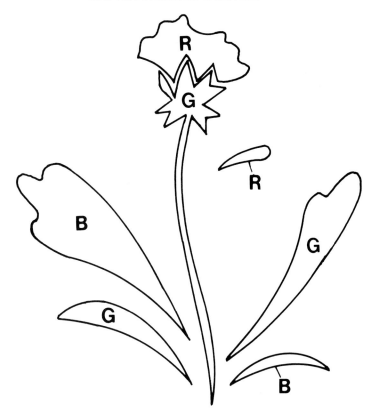

cil, protect other areas of crocheted block by covering with tape or scrap paper.

Stir paint and place about one tablespoon in saucer. Blend in five or six drops of water; if paint appears to be drying, blend in a few more drops of water, keeping paint the consistency of soft butter throughout. To stencil, dip brush into paint, then pounce brush on paper towel until almost dry. (**Note:** It is extremely important that brush not be too wet. Otherwise, pain will seep below surface of yarn and into the fibers beneath.) Holding brush like a pencil, perpendicular to surface, brush over cutout area with a circular motion, working over edge of stencil for a clean line; do not press brush down into fibers of yarn, but work with a light touch, so that paint lies on surface of yarn only. Allow paint to dry, then carefully lift stencil from block; wipe clean with damp paper towel; dry. Wash and dry brushes and saucer thoroughly between color changes.

To fasten colors, first allow paint to dry completely, at least one hour. Use press cloth and iron each side of stenciled block with a back-and-forth motion for one minute.

Handy House Holders

Cute cottage-motif kitchen accessories make great housewarming gifts. Crochet pot holders, casserole mitt, pot handle, hot mat, and egg cozies. Add windows, doors, shutters, and posy-filled flower boxes for a pretty touch.

House Pot Holders

SIZE: 6½″ × 7½″.

MATERIALS: Sport weight cotton yarn, one 50-gram (1.75-oz.) ball each green (A), blue (B), purple (C), pink (D); small amounts of beige (E) and white (F). Crochet hook size 4/E (3.5 mm) or size required to obtain gauge. Tapestry needle.

GAUGE: 5 sc = 1″; 6 rows = 1″.

Pot Holder #1

With A, beg at side edge of house, ch 26.

Row 1: Sc in 2nd-ch from hook and in each ch across—25 sc. Ch 1, turn each row.

Rows 2–6: Sc in each sc.

Row 7 (wrong side): With D, working over A, sc in 12 sc, drop D to wrong side; with A, sc in 13 sc.

Row 8: Sc in 13 sc, change to D, working over A, sc in 12 sc.

Row 9: With D, working over A, sc in 12 sc; with A, sc in 5 sc; with another strand of D, working over A, sc in 6 sc; with A, sc in last 2 sc.

Row 10: With A, sc in 2 sc; with D, working over A, sc in 6 sc; with A, sc in 5 sc; with D, working over A, sc in 12 sc.

Rows 11–14: Repeat rows 9 and 10. Cut last D strand at end of door.

Row 15: With A, sc in 17 sc; with D, working over A, sc in 6 sc; with A, sc in 2 sc.

Row 16: Sc in 2 sc; with D, working over A, sc in 6 sc; with A, sc in 17 sc.

Rows 17–20: Repeat rows 15 and 16.

Row 21: Sc in 5 sc; with D, working over A, sc in 6 sc; with A, sc in 6 sc; with D, working over A, sc in 6 sc; with A, sc in 2 sc.

Row 22: Sc in 2 sc, with D, working over A, sc in 6 sc; with A, sc in 6 sc; with D, working over A, sc in 6 sc; with A, sc in 5 sc.

Rows 23–26: Repeat rows 21 and 22.

Rows 27–32: Continue to work lower window on 6 sc; work all other sc in A. At end of row 32, cut D.

Rows 33–36: Work even in A.

ROOF: With A from right side, work sc in end of each row across roof edge—36 sc. End off; turn.

Row 1 (wrong side): With E, 3 sc in first sc, sc in each sc across to last st, 3 sc in last sc—40 sc. Ch 1, turn each row.

Row 2: Working in back lps only, sc in each sc.

Row 3: Dec 1 sc; working in front lps only, sc in each sc to last 2 sts, dec 1 sc.

Row 4: Dec 1 sc; working in back lps only, sc in each sc.

Rows 5–16: Repeat rows 3 and 4. End off.

CHIMNEY: With A, ch 2.

Row 1: Sc in 2nd ch from hook. Ch 1, turn each row.

Row 2: 2 sc in sc.

Row 3: Sc in first sc, 2 sc in next sc.

Row 4: 2 sc in first sc, sc in 2 sc.

Row 5: Sc in 3 sc, 2 sc in next sc.

Row 6: 2 sc in first sc, sc in 4 sc. Work 2 more rows of 6 sc. End off. Sew shaped edge of chimney to last 6 rows of roof.

TRIMMINGS: With C, sl st across top of windows; work 4 vertical rows of sl sts on upper window and 2 vertical rows on lower window to form window panes. Thread C in tapestry needle; draw yarn horizontally through center of window panes on both windows. With E, ch 7. Work 1 row of 6 sc. Make three more pieces the same. Sew to each side of each window for shutters.

WINDOW BOXES: With B, ch 25.

Row 1 (right side): Sc in 2nd ch from hook and in each ch. End off.

Row 2 (right side): Join F in first sc of row 1; working in back lps only, sc in first 2 sc, * ch 3, sk 1 sc, sc in next sc, repeat from * across, end sc in last 2 sc. End off. Work another window box for lower window on 17 sc. With B, sew window boxes under windows; with F, sew "flowers" in place (see flower instructions under Pot Holder #2).

Embroider or crochet "flowers" with F along bottom of house each side of door (see Embroidery Stitch Details, page 78).

With C, sl st around door. With E, embroider French knot for doorknob.

Pot Holder #2

With E, ch 38.

Row 1 (right side): Sc in 2nd ch from hook and in next 14 ch, change to A, working over E, sc in 7 ch, drop A to wrong side; with E, sc in 15 ch. Ch 1, turn each row.

Rows 2–6: Continue to work 15 E sc each side of door; work 7 sc with A for door, working over E.

Row 7: Sc in 4 sc; with A, working over E, sc in 7 sc; with E, working over A, sc in 4 sc; with A, working over E, sc in 7 sc; with E, working over A, sc in 4 sc; with A, working over E, sc in 7 sc; with E, sc in 4 sc.

Rows 8–12: Continue to work two windows and door with 7 sc of A each as in row 7. Cut A at end of last window on row 12.

Rows 13 and 14: Work as for row 2. Cut A at end of row 14.

Rows 15–20: Work even in E.

Row 21: Sc in 8 sc; with A, working over E, sc in 6 sc; with E, working over A, sc in 9 sc; with A, working over E, sc in 6 sc; with E, sc in 8 sc.

Rows 22–26: Continue to work two windows of 6 sc each, working over A between windows. Cut A at end of 2nd window on row 26.

Rows 27–30: Work even in E.

ROOF: Row 1 (wrong side): With B, working on wrong side, sc in each sc across.

Row 2: Dec 1 sc, sc in back lps of each sc to last 2 sts, dec 1 sc.

Row 3: Dec 1 sc, sc in front lps of each sc to last 2 sts, dec 1 sc. Repeat rows 2 and 3 until 3 sts remain. Pull up a lp in 3 sc, yo and through all lps on hook.

CHIMNEY: With E, ch 2.

Row 1: Sc in 2nd ch from hook. Ch 1, turn each row.

Row 2: 2 sc in sc.

Row 3: Sc in first sc, 2 sc in next sc.

Row 4: 2 sc in first sc, sc in 2 sc.

Row 5: Sc in 3 sc, 2 sc in next sc.

Row 6: 2 sc in first sc, sc in 4 sc. End off. Sew shaped edge of chimney to right side of roof near top.

TRIMMING: With C, ch 37. Sc in 2nd ch from hook, * hdc in next ch, sc in next ch, sl st in next ch, sc in next ch, repeat from * across, end sl st in last ch. Sew trimming along bottom edge of roof.

WINDOW TRIMS: With C, sl st across top, bottom and center of each window. With C in tapestry needle, make a vertical st at center of each window to form panes. With C, ch 8. Sc in 2nd ch from hook and in each ch. End off. Make seven more "shutters." Sew to sides of windows.

DOOR TRIM: With C, ch 37. Sc in 2nd ch from hook and in 12 ch, 2 sc in next ch, sc in next 2 ch, hdc in next ch, dc in next 2 ch, hdc in next ch, sc in next 2 ch, 2 sc in next ch, sc in 13 ch. End off. Sew trim around door. With E, embroider French knot for doorknob (see Embroidery Stitch Details, page 78).

FLOWER (make two): With A, ch 16.

Row 1: Sc in 2nd ch from hook and in each ch. Ch 1, turn.

Row 2: With D, sc in first sc; * with A, sc in next sc; with D, sc in 2 sc; repeat from * across, end with D, sc in last sc. Ch 1, turn.

Row 3: Repeat row 2. End off. With A, sew ch edge to bottom of house on each side of door. With D, sew D sts to house.

POT HOLDER #3

Work as for pot holder #1, using C for house, E for door and windows, A for roof, C for chimney. Work roof trimming in F as for pot holder #2. Make shutters, window and door trims in F, window boxes in A and D, flowers in D.

EGG COZIES/POT HANDLE

SIZE: 3″ × 5½″.

MATERIALS: Sport weight cotton yarn, one 50-gram (1.75-oz.) ball each of purple (A), green (B), beige (C), blue (D), pink (E), white (F). Crochet hook size 4/E (3.5 mm) or size required to obtain gauge. Tapestry needle.

GAUGE: 5 sc = 1″; 6 rows = 1″.

EGG COZY: FRONT: With A, ch. 16.

Row 1: (right side): Sc in 2nd ch from hook and in next 4 ch; with C, working over A, sc in 5 ch; drop C to wrong side; with A, sc in 5 sc. Ch 1, turn each row.

Rows 2–8: With A, sc in each A sc; with C, working over A, sc in each C sc.

Rows 9–12: Work even in A.

Row 13: (With A, sc in 3 sc; with C, working over A, sc in 3 sc) twice; with A, sc in 3 sc.

Rows 14–16: Repeat row 13.

Rows 17–20: Work even in A. Cut A.

Row 21: With F, sc in first sc, * long sc in next st of row 19, sc in next 2 sc, repeat from * across, end sc in last sc. Cut F.

Row 22 (wrong side): With B, sc in front lp of each sc. Ch 1, turn each row.

Row 23: Sc in back lp of each sc.

Row 24: Dec 1 sc, sc in front lp of each sc to last 2 sc, dec 1 sc.

Row 25: Dec 1 sc, sc in back lp of each sc to last 2 sc, dec 1 sc. Repeat last 2 rows until 3 sc remain. Draw up a lp in 3 sc, yo and through all lps on hook. End off.

TRIMMINGS: With F, make a ch long enough to go around each window and door; sew chains in place. Embroider a French knot for doorknob (see Embroidery Stitch Details, page 78). Embroider horizontal and vertical sts in F to form window panes. With B, ch 6. Sc in 2nd ch from hook, hdc in next ch, dc in next ch, hdc in next ch, sc in last ch. End off. Make another piece the same. Sew pieces to bottom of house on each side of door.

BACK: With B, ch 16. Work even on 15 sc for 21 rows. Dec 1 sc each side of each row until 3 sc remain. Draw up a lp in 3 sc, yo and through all lps on hook. End off.

FINISHING: With B, sc front and back tog along sides and top of house, leaving bottom edges open. With A, work 5 sc along one edge of roof for chimney. Work in sc, dec 1 sc at beg of each row until no sts remain.

Make pot handle cover using other colors as desired.

House Hot Mat

SIZE: 12″ × 9″.

MATERIALS: Sport weight cotton yarn, one 50-gram (1.75-oz.) ball each blue (A), beige (B), and white (C); small amounts of pink (D), purple (E), green (F). Crochet hook size 4/E (3.5 mm) or size required to obtain gauge. Tapestry needle.

GAUGE: 5 sc = 1″; 6 rows = 1″.

HOT MAT: With A, ch 61.

Row 1 (right side): Sc in 2nd ch from hook and in next 14 ch; with C, working over A, sc in next 7 ch, drop C; with A, sc in each ch to end. Ch 1, turn each row.

Row 2: Sc in each A sc; with C working over A, sc in 7 sc; with A, sc to end.

Rows 3–5: Repeat row 2. Cut C.

Row 6: With A, sc in 27 sc; (with C, working over A, sc in 7 sc; with A, working over C, sc in 4 sc) twice; with C, working over A, sc in 7 sc; with A, sc in last 4 sc.

Rows 7–11: With A, sc in each A sc; with C, sc in each C sc, working over unused colors as before.

Row 12: With A, sc in 38 sc; with C, sc in 7 sc; cut C; with A, sc in 15 sc.

Rows 13–16: With A, sc in 60 sc.

Row 17: (With A, sc in 4 sc; with C, sc in 7 sc) 3 times; with A, sc in 27 sc.

Rows 18–21: Work A sc in each A sc; with C, sc in each C sc. Cut C.

Rows 22–25: With A, sc in each sc.

Row 26: At end of row 25, sc down side of piece, working sc in end of each row, 3 sc in corner, sc in each st to C sts for door, cut A; join A at opposite side of door, sc in each st to next corner, 3 sc in corner, sc in each row to top, 3 sc in corner, sc in each sc across row 25. End off.

Row 27 (right side): Beg at right edge with B, sc in corner sc and next 41 sc, change to A in last sc, drop B; with A, sc in 21 sc. Ch 1, turn.

Row 28: Sk first sc, sc in 20 sc, change to B in last sc; with B, sc in front lp of each sc to last sc, sk last sc. Ch 1, turn.

Row 29: Sc in back lp of each B sc, work B sc in next sc; with A, sc in both lps of each sc to end.

Row 30: Sk first sc, sc in each A sc, change to B; with B, sc in front lp of each sc across. Ch 1, turn. Continue in this way, dec 1 st at right edge of roof every other row, working roof in ridged effect. Work 1 extra st in B at inner edge of roof every other row, dec 1 st at left edge of house every other row. Work until 1 st of A remains. With A, sc down shaped left edge of house. End off. With B, sc across top of roof and down shaped left edge of house.

CHIMNEY: With A, ch 2.

Row 1: Sc in 2nd ch from hook. Ch 1, turn each row.

Row 2: 2 sc in sc.

Row 3: Sc in first sc, 2 sc in next sc.

Row 4: 2 sc in first sc, sc in 2 sc. Continue in this way, inc 1 st at same edge every row for 4 more rows. End off. Sew shaped edge of chimney to roof.

WINDOWS: With E, sc in each st across top and bottom of each window. With E, ch 9 and ch 6. Sew chains across window to form panes. With D, work 10 pieces of 6 sc for shutters. Sew in place.

DOOR: With D, sc around door. With E, form window on door with sc. Embroider doorknob with French knot (see Embroidery Stitch Details, page 78).

FLOWERS: Work 2 chains with F about 46 ch long. Sew chains to lower edge of each side of door, gathering chains to 3″ width. Embroider extra loops of chains above lower edge with C, D, and E chain sts to form flowers.

TRELLIS: Thread two strands of C in tapestry needle. Form three upright posts of trellis by threading C through horizontal bars of sc every other row from lower edge to row 24, making posts ¾″ apart. With single strand of C, form bars across trellis every 2 rows, stitching around posts to anchor sts.

VINE: With F, ch 10. Sc in 2nd ch from hook and in next ch, hdc in next ch, sk 2 ch, 3 dc in next ch, sk 2 ch, dc in last ch. Ch 7, 3 dc in 3rd ch from hook, (ch 3, 3 dc in 3rd ch from hook) twice, ch 7, sl st in 5th ch from hook, 7 sc in ring. End off. Decorate vine with E, D, and C sts, tacking vine in place on trellis at same time.

Long Hot Mitt

SIZE: 30″ × 7″.

MATERIALS: Sport weight cotton yarn, four 50-gram (1.75-oz.) balls beige (A), one ball each green (B) and blue (C), small amounts of pink (D), white (E) and purple (F). Crochet hook size 4/E (3.5 mm) or size required to obtain gauge.

GAUGE: 5 sc = 1″; 6 rows = 1″.

MITT: With A, ch 13.

Row 1 (right side): Sc in 2nd ch from hook and in each ch across—12 sc. Ch 1, turn.

Row 2: 2 sc in first sc, sc in each of 11 sc. Ch 6, turn.

Row 3: Sc in 2nd ch from hook and in each of next 4 ch, sc in 13 sc—18 sc. Ch 1, turn each row.

Row 4: 2 sc in first sc, sc in each sc across.

Row 5: Sc in each sc across—19 sc.

Row 6: Repeat row 4.

Row 7: Repeat row 5—20 sc.

Row 8: Repeat row 4.

Row 9: 2 sc in first sc, sc in each sc across—22 sc. Repeat row 9 until there are 36 sc. Work even on 36 sc until piece is 27″ from start, end wrong side. Dec 1 sc at beg of every row until 22 sc remain, end wrong side.

Next Row (right side): Dec 1 st at beg of row, sc in each sc across—21 sc.

Next Row: Sc in each sc across. Repeat last 2 rows until 18 sc remain, end wrong side.

Next Row: Dec 1 st at beg of row, sc in each of next 11 sc. Ch 1, turn.

Next Row: Sc in 12 sc. End off.

HOUSE (make 2): Beg at lower edge with C, ch 36. Turn.

Row 1 (wrong side): With A, working over C, sc in 14 ch, change to C in last sc; with C, working over A, sc in 8 ch; change to A, drop C to wrong side; with A, sc in 14 ch. Ch 1, turn each row.

Row 2 (right side): With A, sc in 14 sc, change to C; with C, working over A, sc in 8 sc; change to A, drop C to wrong side; with A, sc in 14 sc.

Row 3: Sc in 14 sc, change to C; with C, working over A, sc in 8 sc, change to A; with A, sc in 14 sc.

Row 4: Repeat row 2. Cut C.

Row 5: With A, sc in 4 sc; with C, working over A, sc in 6 sc, change to A; with A, working over C, sc in 4 sc, change to C; with C, working over A, sc in 8 sc, change to A; with A, working over C, sc in 4 sc, change to C; with C, working over A, sc in 6 sc, drop C to wrong side; with A sc in 4 sc.

Rows 6–14: Continue in this way, working C windows of 6 sc, C door of 8 sc, all other sts in A.

Row 15: Repeat row 2. Cut C.

Rows 16–19: Work even in A.

Row 20 (right side): With A, sc in 5 sc, change to C; working over unused colors as before, work 5 C sc, 5 A sc, 6 C sc, 5 A sc, 5 C sc, 5 A sc.

Rows 21–23: Work A sc in A sc, C sc in C sc. At end of row 23, cut C.

Rows 24–27: With A, sc in each sc. At end of row 27, change to B. Cut A.

Rows 28 and 29: With B, sc in each sc.

Row 30: Dec 1 sc, sc in back lp of each sc to last 2 sc, dec 1 sc.

Row 31: Dec 1 sc, sc in front lp of each sc to last 2 sc, dec 1 sc.

Rows 32–41: Repeat rows 30 and 31—12 sc.

Row 42: Sc in each sc. End off.

TRIMMINGS: With A, embroider French knot for doorknob (see Embroidery Stitch Details, page 78). With A, work a row of sl st around sides and top of door and around each window. With A, make chains for window panes; sew in place. With F, ch 37. Sc in 2nd ch from hook, * hdc in next ch, sc in next ch, sl st in next ch, sc in next ch, repeat from * across, end sl st in last ch. Sew trimming along bottom edge of roof.

SHUTTERS: With F, ch 11. Sc in 2nd ch from hook and in each ch. End off. Make 3 more pieces the same. Sew to sides of downstairs windows.

WINDOW BOXES: With E, ch 8. Sc in 2nd ch from hook and in each sc. Cut E. With B, sc in each sc. Cut B. With D, sl st in each sc. Cut D. Sew a window box under each upstairs window.

CHIMNEY: With A, ch 2.

Row 1: Sc in 2nd ch from hook. Ch 1, turn each row.

Row 2: 2 sc in sc.

Row 3: Sc in first sc, 2 sc in next sc.

Row 4: 2 sc in first sc, sc in 2 sc.

Row 5: Sc in 3 sc, 2 sc in next sc.

Row 6: 2 sc in first sc, sc in 4 sc. Cut A. Sew chimney to roof to correspond to chimney extension at each end of long mitt piece; sew chimney to extension on long piece.

FINISHING: With B, sc roof to shaped end of long piece. With C, sc sides of house to long piece, continuing to edge long piece with C sc when houses have been crocheted on.

Appliance Cozies

Give your kitchen a town 'n' country look with these cheerful crocheted countertop appliance "cozies."

COFFEE MAKER COVER

SIZE: 11″ × 15½″ × 7½″.
MATERIALS: Cotton worsted weight yarn, four 50-gram (1.75-oz.) balls blue (A); two balls white (B); small amounts of black (C), red (D), pink (E), purple (F), and green (G). Crochet hook size 5/F (3.75 mm) or size required to obtain gauge. Tapestry needle.
GAUGE: 4 sts = 1″.
COVER: FRONT: With A, ch 45.

Row 1 (right side): Sc in 2nd ch from hook and in each ch across—44 sc. Ch 2, turn.
Row 2: Hdc in each sc across. Ch 2, turn.
Row 3: Hdc in each hdc across. Ch 2, turn. Repeat row 3 until piece is 12″ from start, end wrong side. Drop A.
Row 1: With B, sc in each hdc across. Drop B.
Row 2: With A, work sc in each sc across. End off A.
Rows 3 and 5: With B, sc in both lps of first sc, sc in front lp of each sc across to last sc, sc in both lps of last sc. Ch 1, turn.
Row 4: Sc in both lps of each sc. Ch 1, turn.

Row 6: (Draw up a lp in next st) twice, yo and through 3 lps on hook (dec made), sc across to last 2 sts, dec 1 sc. Continue to dec 1 sc each side every row for 9 more rows, working wrong-side rows in front lps of sc as in row 3. End off.

BACK: Work as for front.

SIDE PANEL: With A, ch 31. Work as for front on 30 sts without decreasing until piece is 23″ long. Work A and B stripes, then continue in A hdc for 12″, end 1 row sc on right side.

DOOR: With B, beg at side edge, ch 23. Work 10 rows of 22 sc. Ch 1; work 9 sc across short end. Ch 1, turn. Work in sc, dec 1 sc each end for 3 rows—3 sc. Ch 1, sk 1 sc, sc in next sc, sl st in last st. End off. With C, work sc around sides and top of door, working 3 sc in top st of door. With C, embroider line across top of door and 2 rectangular panels on door in backstitch (see Embroidery Stitch Details, page 78).

TOP WINDOWS (make two): With B, beg at side edge, ch 14. Work 14 rows of 13 sc. End off. With C, embroider line between rows 3 and 4 and between rows 11 and 12 in backstitch to mark off shutters; embroider 3 more vertical lines every 2 rows. Embroider 6 horizontal lines to form window panes.

LOWER WINDOWS (make two): With B, beg at side edge, ch 15. Work 14 rows of 14 sc. End off. With C, embroider window panes as for top windows. With D, work 2 rows of 8 sc at bottom edge across window section for window box. With E and F, embroider flowers with G leaves above window box, using straight sts or lazy daisy st (see Embroidery Stitch Details, page 78).

FINISHING: With B, sc pieces tog. Work 1 row of sc around bottom edge. Sew windows and door to front.

MIXER/FOOD PROCESSOR COVER

SIZE: 14″ × 14″ × 8½″.

MATERIALS: Cotton worsted weight yarn, four 50-gram (1.75-oz.) balls green (A); three balls ecru (B); two balls black (C); one ball white (D); small amounts of red (E), pink (F), and purple (G). Crochet hook size 5/F (3.75 mm) or size required to obtain gauge. Tapestry needle.

GAUGE: 4 sts = 1″.

COVER: FRONT: With A, ch 56.

Row 1 (right side): Sc in 2nd ch from hook and in each ch across—55 sc. Ch 2, turn.

Row 2: Hdc in each sc across. Ch 2, turn.

Row 3: Hdc in each hdc across. Ch 2, turn. Repeat row 3 until piece is 8½″ from start, end right side. Change to C. Ch 1, turn.

ROOF: Row 1: With C, sc in each st across. Change to B. Ch 1, turn.

Row 2: With B, sc in each sc across. Ch 1, turn.

Row 3 (wrong side): Sc in front lp of each sc across. Ch 1, turn.

Row 4: Sc in both lps of each sc across. Ch 1, turn. Repeat rows 3 and 4 until piece is 11¼″ from start.

Next Row: (Draw up a lp through next sc) twice, yo and through 3 lps on hook (dec made), sc across to last 2 sts, dec 1 sc. Ch 1, turn. Continue in sc pat, dec 1 sc each side every other row 4 times more. End off. With C, sc around sides and top of piece, working 3 sc in each corner.

BACK: Work as for front.

SIDE PANEL: With A, ch 34. Work as for front on 33 sts until piece is 11¼″ from start. Continue even in rows of sc until piece is 28″ from start, end wrong side. With C, work 1 row sc through both lps. Change to A, work in hdc for 8¼″, end wrong side. Work 1 row sc. End off. With C, sc across both long edges of panel.

DOOR: With B, ch 23. Work in rows of 22 sc for 10 rows. End off. With C, sc around door, working 3 sc in each corner. Join C in top right corner, work sc, hdc, dc, tr, dc, hdc, sc across top. End off. With C, embroider panels on door in backstitch, doorknob in French knot (see Embroidery Stitch Details, page 78).

WINDOWS (make two): With B, ch 15. Work in rows of 14 sc for 3 rows. Change to D, work 8 rows of sc. Change to B, work 3 rows of sc. End off. With C, work 2 rows of 8 sc across one edge of D section. With C, embroider 5 vertical lines in backstitch on each window: one line between B and D sections each side and 3 lines between. Embroider 7 horizontal lines across D section to form window panes. With E, F, and G, embroider flowers with A leaves near bottom of windows, using straight sts or lazy daisy st.

ATTIC WINDOW: With D, ch 13. Work in rows of 12 sc for 10 rows. End off. With C, work 1 row of sc around piece. With C, embroider 5 vertical and 3 horizontal lines on window in backstitch.

FINISHING: Sew windows and door in place. With C, sc pieces tog and sc around bottom edges of cover.

BLENDER COVER

SIZE: 15″ × 8½″ × 8½″.

MATERIALS: Cotton worsted weight yarn, six 50-gram (1.75-oz.) balls ecru (A); one ball each black (B), white (C), green (D), and red (E). Crochet hook size 5/F (3.75 mm) or size required to obtain gauge. Tapestry needle.

GAUGE: 4 hdc = 1″.

COVER: FRONT: With A, ch 34.

Row 1: Sc in 2nd ch from hook and in each ch across—33 sc. Ch 2, turn.

Row 2: Hdc in each sc across. Ch 2, turn.

Row 3: Hdc in each hdc across. Ch 2, turn. Repeat row 3 until piece is 15″ from start. Work 1 row sc all around piece, working 3 sc in each corner. End off.

BACK: Work same as front.

SIDE PANEL: Work same as back, continuing in hdc until piece is 38″ from start, end with 1 row sc. Work 1 row sc all around piece, working 3 sc in each corner. End off.

POTTED TREES (make two): With E, ch 6.

Row 1: Sc in 2nd ch from hook and in next 4 ch—5 sc. Ch 1, turn each row.

Row 2: 2 sc in first sc, sc to last st, 2 sc in last sc—7 sc.

Rows 3 and 4: Sc in each sc. End off.

Row 5: With D, sc in 3 center sc of row 4.

Row 6–8: 2 sc in first sc, sc to last st, 2 sc in last sc—9 sc.

Row 9: Sk first sc, sc to last 2 sts, sk next st, sc in last sc.

Row 10: Sc in each sc.

Rows 11–14: Repeat rows 9 and 10 twice—3 sc.

Row 15: Sk first sc, sc in next sc, sl st in last sc. End off.

DOOR: With B, ch 9.

Row 1: Sc in 2nd ch from hook and in each ch—8 sc. Ch 1, turn each row. Work 19 more rows of 8 sc. End off. Join C in bottom corner, work sc up long side, across top, and down second long side. End off. Join C at upper corner, work 8 sc across top. Ch 1, turn. Work 3 rows of sc, dec 1 st each edge every row—2 sc. End off.

WINDOW (make four): With B, ch 8. Work 2 rows of 7 sc. Change to C, work 15 rows. Change to B, work 2 rows. End off.

FINISHING: Work embroidery on windows, following color photograph. Embroider C cross-stitch on door for doorknob. Embroider C number on door with backstitch (see Embroidery Stitch Details, page 78). Sew windows, door, and trees in place. With B, crochet front, back, and panel tog with 1 row of sc. With B, work 1 row of sc around bottom edge.

PROCESSOR BLADE HOLDER

SIZE: 30″ × 6½″.

MATERIALS: Cotton worsted weight yarn, one 50-gram (1.75-oz.) ball each green (A), white (B), pink (C), purple (D), and black (E). Crochet hook size 5/F

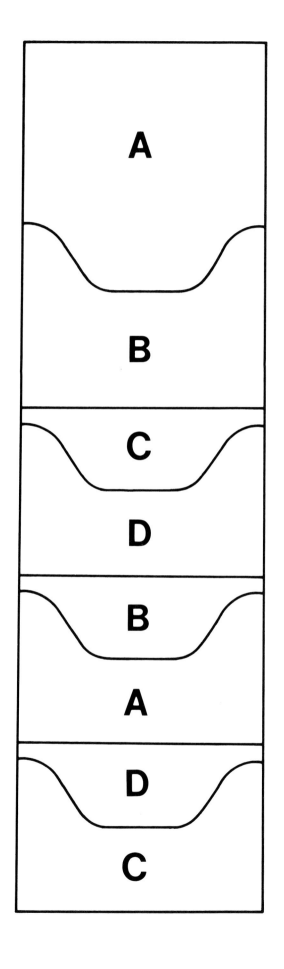

(3.75 mm) or size required to obtain gauge. Dowel, 6½" long.

GAUGE: 4 hdc = 1".
HOLDER: With A, ch 29.
Row 1: Sc in 2nd ch from hook and in each ch across—28 sc. Ch 2, turn.
Row 2: Hdc in each sc across. Ch 2, turn. Continue in hdc, work 29 rows A, 19 rows C, 19 rows B, 19 rows D. End off.
POCKET (make one each A, B, C, and D): Ch 29.
Row 1: Sc in 2nd ch from hook and in each ch across—28 sc. Ch 1, turn each row.
Row 2 (wrong side): Sc in both lps of first sc, sc in front lp only of each st to last st, sc in both lps of last sc.
Row 3: Sc in both lps of each sc.
Rows 4–11: Repeat rows 2 and 3.
Row 12: Keeping to pat, work sc in 12 sts. Ch 1, turn.
Row 13: Sk first st, sc in next st and in each st across.
Row 14: Work to last 2 sts, sk next st, sc in last st. Repeat rows 13 and 14 four times.
Next Row: Sk first st, sc in 2nd st. End off. Leave center 4 sts unworked. Join yarn in 5th st, work 12 sc to end of row. Work as for other side, reversing shaping. With matching color, from right side, sc around pocket, working 3 sc in each corner and at both points. End off. Join E in first sc of right point, 3 sc in point, sc across top of pocket, 3 sc in left point. End off. With E, sc across bottom of pocket. Omit this row on C (bottom) pocket.
FINISHING: Pin pockets to main piece, following diagram on page 40. With E, beg at top left corner of main piece, sc along side edge, joining pockets to main piece, 3 sc in corner, sc across bottom, joining last pocket to main piece, 3 sc in corner, sc to top. With E, sl st bottom of 3 top pockets to main piece. Fold 1½" at top of holder to wrong side and sew hem in place. Insert dowel. Join E at one end of hem, ch 40 for hanger, sl st in other end of hem. End off.

FOUR-SLICE TOASTER COVER

SIZE: 15½" × 8½" × 5½".
MATERIALS: Cotton worsted weight yarn, three 50-gram (1.75-oz.) balls red (A); two balls purple (B); one ball white (C); small amounts of blue (D),

green (E), pink (F), black (G). Crochet hooks sizes 4/E and 5/F (3.5 and 3.75 mm) or sizes required to obtain gauge. Tapestry needle.
GAUGE: 4 sts = 1" (larger hook).
COVER: FRONT: With A and larger hook, ch 63.
Row 1 (right side): Sc in 2nd ch from hook and in each ch—62 sc. Ch 2, turn.
Row 2: Hdc in each sc across. Ch 2, turn.
Row 3: Hdc in each hdc across. Ch 2, turn. Repeat row 3 until piece is 6" from start, end right side. Change to B. Ch 1, turn.
ROOF: Row 1: Sc in first st, sc in front lp only of next st and in each st across to last st, sc in both lps of last st. Ch 1, turn.
Row 2: Sc in both lps of each sc. Ch 1, turn.
Row 3: Sk first sc, sc in next sc, sc in front lp of each sc to last 2 sts, sc in both lps of next sc. Ch 1, turn.
Rows 4–7: Repeat rows 2 and 3.
Row 8: Sc in both lps of each sc. End off.
BACK: Work same as front.
SIDE PANEL: With A and larger hook, ch 22. Work as for front on 21 sts until piece is 6" from start, end right side. Change to B. Repeat rows 1 and 2 of roof until piece is 22" from start, end right side. Change to A, work in hdc for 6", end wrong side. Ch 1, turn. Sc in each hdc. End off.
WINDOWS (make two): With C and larger hook, ch 15. Work 10 rows of 14 sc. Work 1 row of sc around piece, working 3 sc in each corner. End off. With B, work 1 row of sc around piece, working 3 sc in each corner. End off. With G, embroider 3 horizontal and 4 vertical lines in backstitch (see Embroidery Stitch Details, page 78) to form window panes.
DOOR: With B and larger hook, ch 9. Work 19 rows of 8 sc. End off. Join C in bottom corner, sc along long side, 3 sc in corner, sc across short side, 3 sc in corner, sc down second long side. End off. Join C in top corner, work 8 sc across top, sl st in corner. Ch 1, turn. Work in sc for 2 rows, dec 1 st each side of each row. Sl st in each st. End off. With C, embroider square window and rectangular panel on door in backstitch.
FLOWERS (make two D, four F, two E): With smaller hook, ch 6, sl st in first ch to form ring. Work 8 sc in ring. * Ch 5, sc in next sc, repeat from * 4 times—5 petals. End off.
FINISHING: Sew windows and door in place. With C, sc front and back to side panel. Work 1 row sc around bottom of house. Sew flowers to front of house above sc edging.

DECORATIVE SHOW-OFFS

Charm, color, practicality, and ease of creation are all aspects of the varied projects in this group. They offer something for everyone, presenting a miscellany of decorative objects that can make a difference in the way your home "shows off." The selection of gift items ranges from articles that are easy to make to others that are relatively complicated.

Country Boxes

Boxes with a touch of country are practical as well as pretty. Use them to store all sorts of items, from crochet hooks and sewing notions to potpourri. The various shapes and dimensions lend themselves to a variety of uses; there is even a crocheted vase cover.

LARGE OVAL BOX

SIZE: 9″ × 6″ × 4¼″.

MATERIALS: Patons Canadiana, one 100-gram (3.5-oz.) ball each dark teal #41 (A), light rose #11 (B), and rose #14 (C). Crochet hook size 5/F (3.75 mm) or size required to obtain gauge. Two pieces plastic canvas 11″ × 14″. Fabric, ½ yard. Matching sewing thread. Tapestry needle.

GAUGE: 17 sc = 4″; 17 rows = 4″.

Note: When changing colors, work last sc of one color until there are 2 lps on hook; finish sc with new color. Work over strand of dropped color. Carry colors only as far as needed; do not carry unused colors to end of row.

BOX: With A, ch 114.

Row 1: Sc in 2nd ch from hook and in each ch across—113 sc. Ch 1, turn each row.

Row 2: Sc in each sc across.

Row 3: Following Chart 1, work from A to B once, from B to C 5 times, from C to D once.

Row 4: Work from D to C once, from C to B 5 times, from B to A once.

Rows 5–10: Repeat rows 3 and 4.

Work even with A until piece measures 3¾″ from beg. End off. Piece should measure 27″ long. Steam flat. With A, embroider an eye on each pig with French knot (see Embroidery Stitch Details, page 78).

COVER: With C, ch 20.

Rnd 1: Sc in 2nd ch from hook and in next 17 ch, 3 sc in last ch; working back on opposite side of ch, sc in 17 ch, 2 sc in next ch—40 sc. Sl st in first sc.

Rnd 2: Ch 1 (counts as first st), sc in 17 sc, 3 sc in next sc, sc in 18 sc, 3 sc in next sc, sc in last st. Sl st in ch-1 each rnd.

Rnd 3: Ch 1, sc in 18 sc, 3 sc in next st, sc in 20 sc, 3 sc in next st, sc in last 2 sts—48 sc.

Rnd 4: Ch 1, sc in 18 sc, 2 sc in next sc, sc in next sc, 2 sc in next sc, sc in 19 sc, 2 sc in next sc, sc in next sc, 2 sc in next sc, sc in 3 sc—52 sc.

Rnds 5–13: Continue to inc 2 sc each end each rnd, separating incs as necessary to keep work flat—88 sc. End off. Steam piece flat.

Rim: With C, ch 119.

Row 1: Sc in 2nd ch from hook and in each ch—118 sc. Ch 1, turn each row.

Row 2: Following Chart 2, work from A to B once, from B to C 29 times.

Row 3: Work from C to B 29 times, from B to A once.

Rows 4 and 5: Work even with C. End off. Steam piece flat. Weave ends tog. Pin rim around oval cover. With C, sl st rim to cover.

FINISHING: Cut two pieces of plastic canvas 3¾″ × 13½″. Stitch ends tog with yarn to make 3¾″ × 27″ piece. Cut piece of fabric 5″ × 28″. Turn under ½″ on one long and two short edges; hand-sew to back of crocheted piece. Insert plastic between crocheted piece and fabric lining, close last side. Overlap ends about 2″ to form oval, sew ends in place.

For bottom of box, cut plastic same size as crocheted piece; cut two pieces of fabric same as plastic plus ¼″ seam allowance all around. With right sides tog, stitch fabric pieces tog halfway around. Turn right side out, insert plastic and close seam. Hand-sew bottom of box to sides.

For cover, cut plastic and fabric to shape, adding ¼″ seam allowance all around on fabric. Cut two strips of plastic 1″ wide and stitch tog to make 1″ × 25½″ strip. Cut fabric 2″ × 26½″. Stitch plastic rim to plastic top with yarn. With right sides tog, stitch fabric rim to fabric top. Place fabric inside plastic cover and work running stitch along seam to hold lining in place. Place crocheted cover over top of plastic and, folding in fabric edges, stitch crocheted edge of rim to lining.

CHART 1

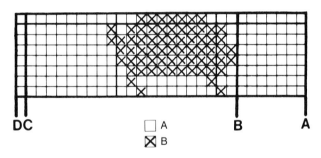

DC   □ A   B   A
        ☒ B

CHART 2

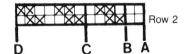

Row 2

D   C   B A

MEDIUM OVAL BOX

SIZE: 8″ × 4¾″ × 3¾″.

MATERIALS: Patons Canadiana, one 100-gram (3.5-oz.) ball each blue #40 (A), yellow #78 (B), and blue mist #38 (C). Crochet hook size 5/F (3.75 mm) or size required to obtain gauge. Two pieces plastic canvas 11″ × 14″. Fabric, ½ yard. Matching sewing thread. Tapestry needle.

GAUGE: 17 sts = 4″; 17 rows = 4″.

Note: When changing colors, work last sc of one color until there are 2 lps on hook; finish sc with new color. Work over strand of dropped color. Carry

CHART 3

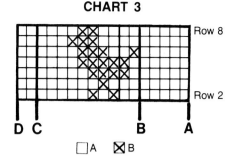

colors only as far as needed; do not carry unused colors to end of row.

BOX: With A, ch 88.

Row 1: Sc in 2nd ch from hook and in each ch—87 sc. Ch 1, turn each row.

Row 2: Following Chart 3, work from A to B once, from B to C 8 times, from C to D once.

Row 3: Work from D to C once, from C to B 8 times, from B to A once.

Rows 4–8: Repeating rows 2 and 3, work to top of chart. Cut B. With A, work even in sc until piece measures 3½". Steam piece flat to measure 3½" × 20". With A, embroider eyes in French knots (see Embroidery Stitch Details, page 78).

COVER: With C, work as for cover of Large Oval Box through rnd 9—72 sc. Steam piece flat.

Rim: With C, ch 85.

Row 1: Sc in 2nd ch from hook and in each ch—84 sc. Change to B. Ch 1, turn.

Row 2: Sc in each sc. Change to A. Ch 1, turn.

Row 3: Sc in each sc. Change to C. Ch 1, turn.

Row 4: Sc in each sc. End off. Steam piece flat. Weave ends tog. Pin rim around oval cover. With C, sl st rim to cover.

FINISHING: Piece tog two strips of plastic canvas 3½" × 10" to form piece 3½" × 20". Cut fabric 4½" × 21". Turn under seam allowance on one long and two short edges; hand-sew to back of crocheted piece. Insert plastic between crocheted piece and fabric lining; close last side. Overlap ends about 1½" to form oval; sew ends in place.

For bottom of box, cut plastic same size as crocheted piece; cut two pieces of fabric same as plastic plus ¼" seam allowance all around. With right sides tog, stitch fabric pieces tog halfway around. Turn right side out, insert plastic and close seam. Hand-sew bottom of box to sides.

For cover, cut plastic and fabric to shape, adding ¼" seam allowance all around on fabric. Cut two strips of plastic for rim 1" wide and stitch tog to make 1" × 20¼" strip. Cut fabric 2" × 21¼". Stitch plastic rim to plastic top with yarn. With right sides tog, stitch fabric rim to top. Place fabric inside plastic cover and work running stitch along seam to hold lining in place. Place crocheted cover over top of plastic, and, folding in fabric edges, stitch crocheted edge of rim to lining.

SMALL OVAL BOX

SIZE: 5¾" × 2¾" × 3".

MATERIALS; Patons Canadiana, one 100-gram (3.5-oz.) ball each light rose #11 (A) and rose #14 (B). Crochet hook size 5/F (3.75 mm) or size required to obtain gauge. Piece of plastic canvas 11" × 14". Fabric, ¼ yard. Matching sewing thread. Tapestry needle.

GAUGE: 17 sc = 4"; 17 rows = 4".

Note: When changing colors, work last sc of one color until there are 2 lps on hook; finish sc with new color. Work over strand of dropped color. Carry colors only as far as needed; do not carry unused colors to end of row.

BOX: With A, ch 63.

Row 1: Sc in 2nd ch from hook and in each ch—62 sc. Ch 1, turn each row.

Row 2: Following Chart 4, work from A to B once, from B to C 6 times, from C to D once.

Row 3: Work from D to C once, from C to B 6 times, from B to A once.

Rows 4–7: Repeat rows 2 and 3. Work even in A until piece measures 3" from beg. End off. Steam piece flat.

COVER: With A, work as for cover of Large Oval Box through rnd 6—60 sc. Steam piece flat.

Rim: With B, ch 57.

Row 1: Sc in 2nd ch from hook and in each ch—56 sc. Ch 1, turn. Following Chart 5, work rows 2–4. End off. Steam piece flat. Weave ends tog. Pin rim around oval cover. With A, sl st rim to cover.

CHART 4

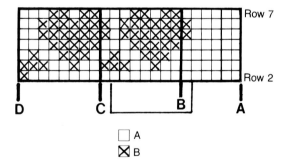

CHART 5

44

FINISHING: Cut plastic 3″ × 14″. Cut fabric 4″ × 15″. Turn under seam allowance on one long edge and two short edges; hand-sew to back of crocheted piece. Insert plastic between crocheted piece and fabric lining; close opening. Overlap ends about 1″ to form oval; sew ends in place.

For bottom of box, cut plastic same size as crocheted piece. Cut 2 pieces of fabric same as plastic plus ¼″ seam allowance all around. With right sides tog, stitch fabric pieces tog halfway around. Turn right side out, insert plastic and close seam. Hand-sew bottom of box to sides.

For cover, cut plastic and fabric to shape, adding seam allowance all around on fabric. Cut 2 strips of plastic for rim 1″ wide and stitch tog to make 1″ × 14½″ strip. Cut fabric 2″ × 15½″. Stitch plastic rim to plastic top with yarn. With right sides tog, stitch fabric rim to top. Place fabric inside plastic cover and work running stitch along seam to hold lining in place. Place crocheted cover over top of plastic and, folding in fabric edges, stitch crocheted edge of rim to lining.

VASE COVER

SIZE: 11″ high × 3″ diameter.
MATERIALS: Patons Canadiana, one 100-gram (3.5-oz.) ball each yellow #78 (A), cranberry #13 (B), dark gold #84 (C), dark teal #41 (D). Crochet hook size 6/G (4.25 mm) or size required to obtain gauge.
GAUGE: 9 sc = 2″; 5 rnds = 1″.
COVER: Beg at center bottom with A, ch 2.
Rnd 1: 6 sc in 2nd ch from hook. Sl st in first sc.
Rnd 2: Ch 1, 2 sc in each sc around. Sl st in first sc—12 sc.
Rnd 3: Ch 1, sc in first sc, * 2 sc in next sc, sc in next sc, repeat from * around, end 2 sc in last sc—18 sc. Join each rnd.
Rnd 4: Ch 1, * sc in 2 sc, 2 sc in next sc, repeat from * around—24 sc.
Rnds 5–8: Continue to inc 6 sc evenly spaced each rnd—48 sc. Cut A.
Rnd 9: With B, sc in each sc around.
Rnd 10: Sc in back lp of each sc around.
Rnds 11 and 12: Sc in each sc around.
Rnd 13: Change to A, * sc in 2 sc, long sc in next sc 2 rnds below, repeat from * around.
Rnds 14 and 15: Sc in each st around.
Rnd 16: Change to C, long sc in first sc 2 rnds below, * sc in 2 sc, long sc in next sc 2 rnds below, repeat from * around, end sc in last 2 sc.
Rnds 17 and 18: Sc in each st around.
Rnds 19–21: Change to A, repeat rnds 13–15.
Rnds 22–24: Change to D, repeat rnds 16–18.

Rnd 25: Change to A, repeat rnd 13. Work even in A for 5″. With D, repeat rnds 16–18. With A, repeat rnds 13–15. With C, repeat rnds 16–18. With A, repeat rnds 13–15. With B, repeat rnds 16–18.
Last Rnd: With B, working from left to right, sc in each sc around (corded edge st). Join; end off.

SQUARE BOX

SIZE: 5½″ × 5½″ × 5½″.
MATERIALS: Patons Canadiana, one 100-gram (3.5-oz.) ball each blue #40 (A), dark gold #84 (B), off-white #94 (C), and cranberry #13 (D). Crochet hook size 5/F (3.75 mm) or size required to obtain gauge. Fabric, ½ yard. Batting 1″–1¼″ thick, ¼ yard. Sewing thread to match fabric. Tapestry needle.
GAUGE: 17 sc = 4″; 17 rows = 4″.
SQUARE 1 (make twelve): With A, ch 2.
Row 1: 2 sc in 2nd ch from hook. Ch 1, turn each row.
Row 2: 2 sc in each sc—4 sc.
Row 3: 2 sc in first st, sc to last st, 2 sc in last st—6 sc.
Rows 4–8: Repeat row 3—16 sc. Finish last sc of row 8 with B. Cut A. Ch 1, turn.
Row 9: With B, sc in each sc. Ch 1, turn each row.
Row 10: Sk first sc, sc in next sc, sc to last 2 sts, sk next st, sc in last st—14 sc.
Rows 11–16: Repeat row 10—2 sc.
Row 17: Sc in 2nd sc. Cut B, pull end through lp. With D, work 1 rnd sc around square, working 3 sc in each corner.
SQUARE 2 (make twelve): Work as for square 1, working rows 1–8 with C, rows 9–17 with D. Do not cut yarn; turn. Work 1 rnd sc around square, working 3 sc in each corner.
LARGE SQUARES (make six): Position 4 squares as in following diagram. With D, sl st squares tog through back lps only. Steam piece flat.

Cut 6 pieces of fabric 6″ square. Cut 6 pieces of batting 5″ square. Pin batting square between fabric and crocheted squares. With tapestry needle and matching yarn, work running stitch through all layers along diagonal lines. Sew a piece of yarn through center of square and tie a knot on right side. Fold edges of fabric under batting and sew fabric to crochet with thread, leaving sc edge exposed all around.
FINISHING: With D, sl st 4 squares tog in one strip for sides of box, working through both lps. Sl st bottom square to sides, then sl st last 2 sides tog to form box. Join D to a top corner, * sc to last st before next corner, draw up a lp in next 2 sts, yo and through 3 lps on hook, repeat from * around. Sl

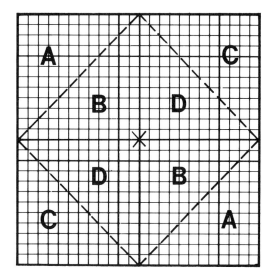

st in first st; end off. With D, sc around last square for top, working 3 sc in each corner. Sl st one edge to back of box.

CYLINDER

SIZE: 6¾″ high × 3″ diameter.

MATERIALS: Patons Canadiana, one 100-gram (3.5-oz.) ball each blue mist #38 (A) and blue #41 (B); small amounts of cranberry #13 (C) and off-white #94 (D) for embroidery. Crochet hook size 5/F (3.75 mm) or size required to obtain gauge. Plastic canvas: one piece 11″ × 14″; two 2⅞″ circles. Fabric, ½ yard. Tapestry needle.

GAUGE: 17 sc = 4″; 17 rows = 4″.

BOX: With A, ch 39.

Row 1: Sc in 2nd ch from hook and in each ch—38 sc. Ch 1, turn each row.

Row 2: Sc in each sc across. Repeat row 2 until piece measures 6¼″. Piece should measure 8½″ wide. Press piece. Following Chart 6, embroider design in cross-stitch (see Embroidery Stitch Details, page 78).

COVER: With B, ch 4. Sl st in first ch to form ring.

Rnd 1: Ch 1, 8 sc in ring. Sl st in first sc.

Rnd 2: Ch 1, 2 sc in each sc around—16 sc. Sl st in first sc each rnd.

Rnd 3: Ch 1, (sc in sc, 2 sc in next sc) 8 times—24 sc.

Rnd 4: Ch 1, (sc in 2 sc, 2 sc in next sc) 8 times—32 sc.

Rnds 5–8: Continue to inc 8 sc evenly spaced each rnd—64 sc. End off.

Rim: With B, ch 46.

Row 1: Sc in 2nd ch from hook and in each ch—45 sc. Ch 1, turn each row.

Rows 2–4: Sc in each sc across. End off. Following Chart 7, embroider rim in cross-stitch. Pin rim to cover, easing to fit. Sl st rim to cover.

FINISHING: Cut plastic 6¼″ × 9½″. Cut fabric 7½″ × 10½″. Place fabric right side out behind plastic. Fold edges over plastic, pin in place. With fabric side facing, work row of running stitch around all edges. Trim two rounds off one plastic circle for base of box. Trace shape on fabric and cut two pieces, adding ¼″ seam allowance all around. With right sides tog, stitch circles tog halfway around; turn right side out. Insert plastic and complete

CHART 6

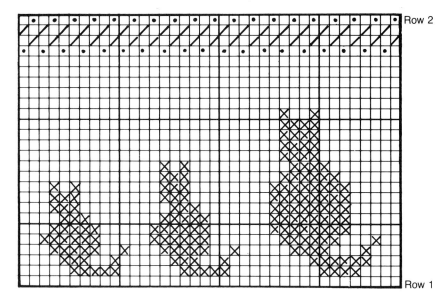

CHART 7

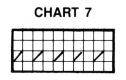

☐ A   ☒ B   ⊡ C   ◩ D

stitching. Stitch base to lined plastic so that fabric is inside cylinder. Overlap edges, pin to hold. Wrap crocheted piece around cylinder and weave edges tog. With thread, stitch crochet to lining around top and bottom.

For cover, trace plastic circle on fabric. Cut shape, adding ¼″ seam allowance. Cut fabric rim 1¼″ × 10½″. With right sides tog, stitch fabric rim to fabric circle. Cut plastic rim ¾″ × 9½″. Stitch plastic rim to plastic circles with yarn.

With right sides tog, stitch fabric rim to fabric top. Place fabric inside plastic cover and work running stitch along seam to hold lining in place. Place crocheted cover over top of plastic and, folding in fabric edges, stitch crochet edge of rim to lining.

Welcome Wreaths

Add a touch of romance to a decorative grapevine wreath or basket with lovely crocheted embellishments in your choice of rosebuds, fans, birds, or filet heart. Arrange and glue dried flowers for a welcome display that can be enjoyed all year long.

HEART BASKET WALLPIECE

SIZE: 13″ × 15″.

MATERIALS: Coats and Clark "Big Ball," size 30, Art. B. 34, one ball each yellow (A), pink (B), white (C), and blue (D). Steel crochet hook No. 8 (1.25 mm). One dozen each white, pale pink, and purple dried flowers. Large bunch dried wheat. Hot glue gun. Heart basket 13″ × 15″. Fabric stiffener. Small piece white fabric. Small amount stuffing.

BIRD

BODY: With A, ch 6; join with sl st to form ring.
Rnd 1: Ch 3, 12 dc in ring; join with sl st to top of ch-3.
Rnd 2: Ch 3, * 2 dc in next st, dc in next st, repeat from * around—18 dc; join with sl st to top of ch-3.
Rnd 3: Ch 3, dc in each st around; join.
Rnd 4: Ch 3, * dc in 3 dc, sk 1 st, repeat from * around—12 dc; join.
Rnd 5: Sc in each st around, sl st in first sc.
Rnds 6 and 7: Repeat rnd 2.
Rnds 8–11: Repeat rnd 3.
Rnd 12: Repeat rnd 4. Do not fasten off.
TAIL: Ch 3, dc in next st, ch 2, 2 dc in same st, sk 2 sts, (2 dc, ch 2, 2 dc) in next st (shell), sk 2 sts, shell in next st. Repeat last row twice. Fasten off.
WING (make two): Ch 6; join with sl st to form ring.
Row 1: (Ch 3, dc, ch 2, 2 dc) in ring, shell in ring; turn.
Rows 2 and 3: (Ch 3, 2 dc, ch 2, 3 dc) in ch-2 sp of first shell, (3 dc, ch 2, 3 dc) in sp of next shell; turn at end of each row.
Rows 4 and 5: (Ch 3, 3 dc, ch 2, 4 dc) in sp of first shell, (4 dc, ch 2, 4 dc) in sp of next shell.
Row 6: Repeat row 2.
Row 7: Repeat row 1, working ch 1 instead of ch 2. Fasten off.
FINISHING: Saturate body and wings with fabric stiffener. As body is drying, shape into rounded form by inserting plastic wrap or other material; fan out tail. Glue wings to body.

ROSEBUD

Make four each A, B, and C:
Row 1: Ch 10, dc in 5th ch from hook and in each ch across. Ch 3, turn.
Rows 2–6: Dc in each st across. Ch 3, turn each row. At end of row 6, ch 3, do not turn.
Row 7: Working along side edge of piece, work 5 dc evenly spaced across.
Rows 8 and 9: Repeat row 2.
Rows 10 and 11: Repeat rows 7 and 8.
Rows 12–14: Repeat row 2.
Rows 15 and 16: Repeat rows 7 and 8.
Rows 17–19: Repeat row 2.
Rows 20 and 21: Repeat rows 7 and 8.
Rows 22–24: Repeat row 2. Fasten off.
FINISHING: Saturate piece with fabric stiffener. When almost dry, beg with row 24, roll up entire piece with points facing outward. Allow to dry completely.

FAN

Make two: With B, ch 8, join with sl st to form ring.
Row 1: Ch 3, 13 dc in ring; turn each row.
Row 2: Ch 4 (counts as dc and ch 1), sk first dc, (dc, ch 1) in each st across—14 dc.
Row 3: Ch 5 (counts as dc and ch 2), sk first dc (dc, ch 2) in each st across, end dc in last dc—14 dc and 13 ch-2 sps.
Row 4: Ch 3, dc in first ch-2 sp, ch 2, 2 dc in same sp, * sk 1 sp, (2 dc, ch 2, 2 dc—shell) in next sp, repeat from * across—7 shells.
Row 5: Ch 3, 2 dc in first ch-2 sp, ch 2, 3 dc in same sp, (3 dc, ch 2, 3 dc) in each ch-2 sp across.
Row 6: Ch 3, 3 dc in first ch-2 sp, ch 2, 4 dc in same sp, (4 dc, ch 2, 4 dc) in each sp across.
Row 7: Ch 3, 4 dc in first sp, ch 2, 5 dc in same sp, (5 dc, ch 2, 5 dc) in each sp across.
Row 8: Ch 3, 5 dc in first sp, ch 2, 6 dc in same sp, (6 dc, ch 2, 6 dc) in each sp across. Fasten off.
FINISHING: Saturate piece with fabric stiffener; dry flat.

FILET HEART

Make two: With D, ch 51.
Row 1: Dc in 6th ch from hook (counts as dc, ch 2 and dc), * ch 2, sk 2 ch, dc in next ch, repeat from * across—17 dc, 16 ch-2 sps. Ch 5 (counts as dc and ch 2), turn.
Row 2: Dc in first dc, (2 dc in sp, dc in next dc) 15 times, ch 2, dc in 3rd ch of ch-5. Ch 5, turn.
Row 3: Sk first dc, dc in next 4 dc, (ch 2, sk 2 dc, dc in next dc) 14 times, 2 dc in sp, dc in 3rd ch of ch-5, ch 5, sl st in bottom of last dc, sl st in 3rd ch of ch-5. Ch 5, turn.

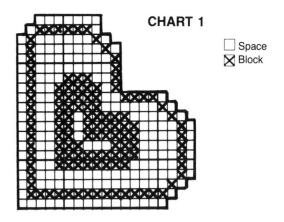

CHART 1

☐ Space
☒ Block

Row 4: Dc in first dc, 2 dc in sp, dc in next dc, (ch 2, dc in next dc) 15 times, dc in next 3 dc, ch 2, sl st in 3rd ch of ch-5. Ch 5, turn.
Rows 5–20: Follow Chart 1, working dc, ch 2, for each space (sp), 3 dc for each block (bl). To dec at end of row, work to within sps or bls to be dec, turn work. To dec at beg of row, sl st across sts to be dec.
EDGING: Row 1: With wrong sides tog, sc hearts tog along straight edges on both sides of points. Continue to sc along top edge of front heart to beg of joining; sc along top edge of back heart.
Row 2: Working along joined section, * sc in 3 sc, ch 3, sk 2 sts, repeat from * along joined section, top edge of front, and top edge of back.
Row 3: [Sc, ch 1, (dc, ch 1) 3 times, sc, ch 1] in each ch-3 sp.
FINISHING: Place crocheted heart on doubled fabric; cut 2 heart pieces with ¼" seam allowance all around.

With right sides tog, sew fabric pieces tog, leaving 2" opening at top. Turn to right side. Stuff with batting; close opening.

Place fabric heart inside crocheted heart. Make a chain about 12" long. Sl through center top of heart to tie to basket.

ASSEMBLY: With hot glue gun, affix dried wheat to inside lower half of basket. Glue on dried flowers, rosebuds, fans, and bird. Tie heart to inside top of basket.

FLOWER WREATH

SIZE: 12" diameter.
MATERIALS: Coats and Clark "Big Ball," size 30, Art. B. 34, one ball each variegated yellow (A), purple (B), and green (C). Steel crochet hook No. 9 (1 mm). White satin ribbon ¹⁄₁₆" wide, 1¾ yards. Cream satin ribbon ⅝" wide, 1½ yards. Grapevine wreath, 10" diameter. Large bunch glycerin-treated baby's breath. Seven gold dried straw flowers. Nine

bunches small dried purple flowers. Fine florist's wire. Hot glue gun. Spray starch.

PANSIES (make twelve each A and B): Ch 6; join with sl st to form ring.

Rnd 1: Ch 3, dc in ring, (ch 4, 2 dc in ring) 4 times, ch 4, sl st in top of ch-3.

Rnd 2: (2 sc, 9 dc, 2 sc) in each ch-4 sp around, sl st in first ch-4 sp to join.

Rnd 3: (make two back petals): (Ch 5, hold ch in back of work and sl st to bottom of front petal) twice. Turn work.

Rnd 4: Working in ch-5 sps of 2 back petals, (2 sc, 9 dc, 2 sc) in each ch-5 sp. Turn work.

Rnd 5: Working on back petals, * sc in first st, (ch 1, sc in next st) acros petal, sl st to next back petal, repeat from * across second back petal.

Rnd 6: Sl st to petal directly in front of petal just worked, repeat rnd 5 across all front petals. End off.

Spray starch and press pansy.

RIBBON: With C, ch 6.

Row 1: Dc in 4th ch from hook, ch 2, sk next ch, 2 dc in last ch. Turn.

Row 2: Sl st to ch-2 sp, ch 3, dc in sp, ch 2, 2 dc in sp. Turn. Repeat row 2 until piece measures 1½ yards. Weave ¹⁄₁₆″ ribbon through ch-2 sps. Spray lightly with starch.

FINISHING: With hot glue gun, affix small bunches of baby's breath to grapevine wreath, completely covering front and sides. Glue dried and crocheted flowers to wreath.

Hold crocheted ribbon and cream ribbon tog;

loop around 5″ cardboard five or six times, remove cardboard, fasten florist's wire in center to secure loops. Glue to bottom of wreath.

Twist a few strands of florist's wire tog; sl through grapevine wreath; twist all strands tog to form ring for hanging.

For the Man in Your Life

Appliqué, stenciling, and embroidery added to a crocheted background provide variety and texture to accent pieces suitable for display in the den or library. The rug, rocker pad, and afghan are just starters. You can use these same techniques to create chair pads, footstool covers, and even basket covers.

ROCKER CUSHIONS

SIZE: Back Cushion: 16″ wide at lower edge, 20″ wide at top, 27″ long. **Seat Cushion:** 15″ wide at front edge, 10″ wide at back edge, 18″ long.

MATERIALS: Bernat Berella "4," four 100-gram (3.5-oz.) balls each yellow #8900 (A) and hunter green #8981N (B); one ball each walnut #8916 (C), brown #8918 (D), camel #8917 (E), medium gold #8885 (F), and copper #8955 (G). Crochet hook size 8/H (5 mm) or size required to obtain gauge. Tapes-try needle. Fiberfill for stuffing. Green seam binding, 4 yards.

GAUGE: 7 sc = 2″; 4 rows = 1″ (sc).
7 sts = 2″; 3 rows = 1″ (sc, dc pat).

SEAT CUSHION

Top: Beg at front edge with A, ch 52.

Row 1: Sc in 2nd ch from hook and in each ch across—51 sc. Ch 1, turn each row.

Row 2: Sc in each sc. Repeat row 2 until piece measures 11″ from beg.

Next Row: Sk first st, sc in each sc across. Ch 1, turn. Repeat last row for 23 rows.

Edging: Rnd 1: From right side, sc around piece, working 3 sc in each corner. Sl st in first sc.

Rnd 2: Ch 1; working from left to right, sc in each sc around (crab st). Join, end off.

Back: With (B), ch 51.

Row 1: Sc in 2nd ch from hook, * dc in next ch, sc in next ch, repeat from * across, end dc in last ch—50 sts. Ch 1, turn.

Row 2: * Sc in dc, dc in sc, repeat from * across. Ch 1, turn. Repeat row 2 until piece is 11″ from start.

Next Row: Sk first st, dc in sc, work in pat across. Repeat last row, end sc in dc.

Next Row: Sk first st, sc in dc, work in pat across, end sc in dc. Repeat last row, end dc in sc. Continue to dec 1 st at beg of each row for 16 more rows. Work edging as for top piece.

CATTAIL: (make three): With C, ch 4. Sc in 2nd ch from hook and in each remaining ch—3 sc. Ch 1, turn each row. Work even on 3 sc until piece measures 3″ from beg. Ch 1, turn. Pull up a lp in each sc, yo and through all lps on hook. End off. Sew cattails to top piece, following chart. With F, sl st to make stems. With B and D, work lines of sl st for reeds.

FINISHING: Cut two 1-yard lengths of seam binding. Sew center of each piece to wrong side of back piece at each back corner. Sew top and back pieces tog inside crab st edging, filling cushion with fiberfill before closing last steam.

BACK CUSHION

Front: Beg at lower edge with A, ch 56. Work as for top seat cushion on 55 sc until piece measures 8″ from beg. Inc 1 st each side of next row, then every 5″ until piece measures 27″ from beg—63 sc. Work edging as for seat cushion.

Back: With B, ch 55. Work as for back seat cushion until piece measures 8″ from beg. Keeping to pat, inc 1 st each side of next row, then every 5″ until piece is same length as front. Work edging as for seat cushion.

DUCK: Note: When changing colors, pull up a lp in last st of one color, drop color to wrong side, finish sc with new color. With C, ch 27.

Row 1: With C, sc in 2nd ch from hook and in next 16 ch; with G, sc in 9 ch. Ch 1, turn each row.

Row 2: Sc in 8 sc; with C, sc in 17 sc.

Row 3: Sk first sc, sc in 16 sc; with G, sc in 5 sc, sk next sc, sc in last sc.

Row 4: Sc in 6 sc; with C, sc in 14 sc, sk next sc, sc in last sc.

Row 5: Sc in 17 sc; with G, sc in 4 sc, 2 sc in last sc.

Row 6: 2 sc in first sc, sc in 5 sc; with C, sc in 17 sc.

Row 7: Sc in 17 sc; with G, sc in 6 sc, 2 sc in last sc.

Row 8: 2 sc in first sc, sc in 7 sc; with C, sc in 17 sc.

Row 9: 2 sc in first sc, sc in 8 sc; with E, sc in 7 sc; with C, sc in 3 sc; with G, sc in 7 sc.

Row 10: Sk first sc, sc in 8 sc, with C, sc in next sc; with E, sc in 10 sc; with C, sc in 6 sc, 2 sc in last sc.

Row 11: Sc in 6 sc; with E, sc in 15 sc; with G, sc in 6 sc.

Row 12: Sk first sc, sc in 6 sc; with E, sc in 14 sc; with C, sc in 5 sc, 2 sc in last sc.

Row 13: With D, sc in first sc; with C, sc in 5 sc; with D, sc in next sc; with E, sc in 15 sc; with G, sc in 3 sc, sk next sc, sc in last sc.

Row 14: Sc in 5 sc; with E, sc in 15 sc; with D, sc in 5 sc, 2 sc in last sc.

Row 15: 2 sc in first sc, sc in 6 sc; with E, sc in 15 sc; with G, sc in 4 sc, 2 sc in next sc. Cut G.

Row 16: With B, sc in 8 sc; with E, sc in 13 sc; with D, sc in 8 sc.

Row 17: Sc in 8 sc; with E, sc in 13 sc. Ch 1, turn.

Row 18: Sc in 10 sc; with D, sc in 3 sc; with E, sc in next sc; with D, sc in 7 sc.

Row 19: Sc in 7 sc; with E, sc in next sc; with D, sc in 3 sc. Ch 1, turn.

Row 20: Sk first sc, sc in 10 sc. End off D. Sk 1 st on row 18, join E in next st, sc in 8 sc. Ch 1, turn. Sk first st, sc in 7 sc. End off E.

Sk 1 st on row 16, join B in next st.

Row 17: Working with B only, sc in 7 sc.

Row 18: 2 sc in first st, sc in 4 sc, sk 1 sc, sc in last sc.

Row 19: Sk first sc, sc in 5 sc, 2 sc in last sc.

Row 20: 2 sc in first sc, sc in 5 sc.

Row 21: 2 sc in first sc, sc in 5 sc, 2 sc in last sc.

Row 22: 2 sc in first sc, sc in 7 sc, 2 sc in last sc.

Row 23: 2 sc in first sc, sc in 10 sc.

Row 24: Sc in 12 sc.

Row 25: Sk first sc, sc in 11 sc.

Row 26: Sk first sc, sc in 8 sc, sk next sc, sc in last sc.

Row 27: Sk first sc, sc in 6 sc, sk next sc, sc in last sc. End off.

Sew duck to top back piece with lower edge of duck at row 18, centering duck on width of piece. With F, embroider beak in satin stitch. With D, make French knot for eye (see Embroidery Stitch Details, page 78). Make 3 cattails as for seat cushion; sew to piece. With F, sl st from duck's back to each cattail. Work sl st reeds in B and D.

FINISHING: Cut two 1-yard lengths of seam binding. Sew center of each piece to wrong side of back piece at each top corner. Sew top and back pieces tog inside crab st edging, filling cushion with fiberfill before closing last seam.

OVAL RUG

SIZE: 44″ × 28″.

MATERIALS: Bernat Berella "4," four 100-gram (3.5-oz.) balls each hunter green #8981N (A) and yellow #8900 (B), one ball each copper #8955 (C) and medium gold #8885 (D). Wooden crochet hook size 13/M or size required to obtain gauge.

GAUGE: 4 sts = 2″; 5 rows = 2″ (double strand of yarn).

RUG: With double strand of A, ch 28.

Rnd 1: Sc in 2nd ch from hook and in next 25 ch, 3 sc in last ch; working back along opposite side of starting ch, sc in 25 ch, 2 sc in same ch as first sc, sl st in first sc. Ch 1, turn.

Rnd 2: 2 sc in each of first 3 sc, sc in 25 sc, 2 sc in each of next 3 sc, sc in 25 sc, sl st in first sc. Ch 1, turn.

Rnd 3: Sc in first sc, sc in each of next 25 sc, 2 sc in each of next 5 sc around end, sc in each of next 26 sc, 2 sc in each of next 5 sc around end, sl st in first sc. Cut 1 strand A, add 1 strand B. Ch 1, turn.

Rnd 4: With A and B, sc in each sc around. Join in first sc, ch 1, turn each rnd.

Rnds 5, 7 and 9: Sc around, inc 6 sc evenly spaced around each end.

Rnds 6 and 8: Work even in sc.

Rnd 10: Repeat rnd 6. Cut A, add another strand B.

Rnds 11, 13 and 17: With 2 strands of B, sc around, inc 6 sc evenly spaced around each end.

Rnd 12: Work even in sc.

Rnds 14–16: Repeat rnd 12.

Rnd 18: Repeat rnd 12. Cut B. Join 2 strands A.

Rnds 19 and 21: With 2 strands A, sc around, inc 6 sc evenly spaced around each end (inc in every 3rd st).

Rnds 20, 22 and 24: Work even in sc.

Rnd 23: Inc 6 sc evenly spaced around each end (inc in every 4th st).

Rnd 25: Inc 6 sc evenly spaced around each end (inc in every 5th st). Cut 1 strand A, join 1 strand B.

Rnd 26: With A and B, inc 6 sc evenly spaced around each end (inc in every 6th st).

Rnds 27 and 29: Work even in sc.

Rnds 28 and 30: Inc 6 sc evenly spaced around each end (inc in every 7th st).

Rnd 31: Repeat rnd 27. End off.

FINISHING: Block rug flat with steam iron. With single strand of C, work a row of sl st between rnds

3 and 4, between rnds 18 and 19, and in last rnd of rug. With D, work a row of sl st between rnds 10 and 11 and between rnds 25 and 26.

MALLARD AFGHAN

SIZE: 54" × 60", plus fringe.
MATERIALS: Bernat Berella "4", ten 100-gram (3.5-oz.) balls each yellow #8900 (A) and hunter green #8981N (B); 1 ball copper #8955 (C). Crochet hook size 9/I (51.5 mm) or size required to obtain gauge.
GAUGE: 7 sc = 2"; 4 rows = 1" (A piece).
  6 sts = 2"; 11 rows = 4" (B piece).
AFGHAN: BLOCK A (make ten): With A, ch 49.
Row 1: Sc in 2nd ch from hook and in each ch across—48 sc. Ch 1, turn each row.
Rows 2–48: Sc in each sc across. End off. Check gauge; piece should measure 13¼" wide, 12" long.
BLOCK B (make ten): With B, ch 41.
Row 1: Sc in 2nd ch from hook, * dc in next ch, sc in next ch, repeat from * across, end dc in last ch—40 sts. Ch 1, turn.
Row 2: * Sc in dc, dc in sc, repeat from * across. Ch 1, turn.
Rows 3–33: Repeat row 2. End off. Check gauge; piece should measure 13¼" wide, 12" long.

STENCILING

EQUIPMENT: Masking tape. Craft knife. Stencil brushes, at least one for each color paint. Small jars with lids. Saucer for palette. Paper towels. Old newspapers. Brown paper. Iron. Press cloth.
MATERIALS: Accent® Country Colors® Stencil #207 or cut your own stencil using actual-size pattern given. Accent® Acrylic Country Colors™ paint, one small jar each #2436 raw sienna (A), #2423 Pennsylvania clay (B), #434 mustard seed (C), #2447 soft black (D), #2444 deep forest green (E), and #2449 Jo Sonja red (F).
DIRECTIONS: Read all directions below and those with stencils and test paints on a sample swatch of crochet before beginning work.
  Cover work surface with newspapers, then brown paper; tape in place. Tape crocheted Block A on top with edges square. Remove pre-cut sections of design from store-bought stencils, following manufacturer's directions (or cut out lettered areas of stencil provided); carefully trim any rough edges with craft knife. Peel away protective backing from stencils and discard. Do not discard Stencil Guard™ included in package, but reserve for storing stencils. Center duck motif on crocheted Block A with sticky side down; press in place (or tape if

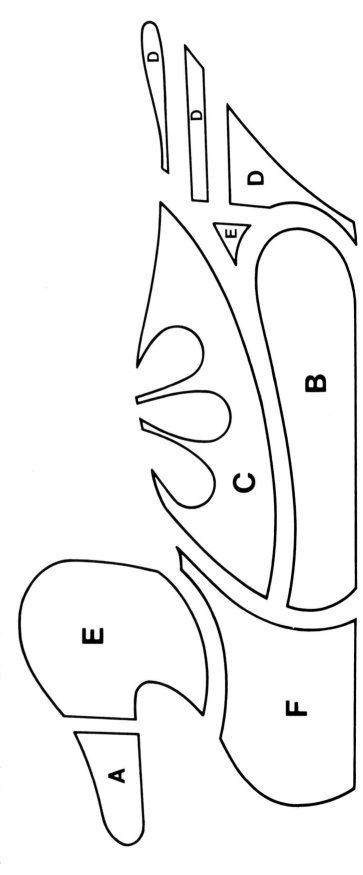

using paper stencil). Do not move stencil while working, or paint will smear.

Stencil each color on design, following illustration for colors. When working on one area of stencil, protect other areas of crocheted block by covering with tape or scrap paper.

Stir paint and place about one tablespoon in saucer. Blend in five or six drops of water; if paint appears to be drying, blend in a few more drops of water, keeping paint the consistency of soft butter throughout. To stencil, dip brush into paint, then pounce brush on paper towel until almost dry. (**Note:** It is extremely important that brush not be too wet. Otherwise, paint will seep below surface of yarn and into the fibers beneath.) Holding brush like a pencil, perpendicular to surface, brush over cutout area with a circular motion, working over edge of stencil for a clean line; do not press brush down into fibers of yarn, but work with a light touch, so that paint lies on surface of yarn only. Allow paint to dry, then carefully lift stencil from block; wipe clean with damp paper towel; dry. Wash and dry brushes and saucer thoroughly between color changes.

To fasten colors, first allow paint to dry completely, at least one hour. Use press cloth and iron each side of stenciled block with a back-and-forth motion for one minute.

FINISHING: Join pieces in checkerboard fashion, four pieces wide by five pieces long. To join, hold two pieces with right sides tog, sew edges tog with overcast st. With B, work 1 row sc across bottom and top edges of afghan.

Fringe: Cut B into 8" lengths. Using 2 strands for each fringe, knot a fringe in each sc across bottom and top edges.

Sl st trimming: With C, work a row of sl st across both ends of afghan and across all seams.

Quilt Motifs in Crochet

An antique Amish quilt is the inspiration for these handsome and homey crocheted accents. Create an afghan, wall hanging, and matching pillows featuring appliqué motifs taken from the quilt patterns.

SIZES: Afghan, 42" × 55"; wall hanging, 28" square; pillow, 12" square.

MATERIALS: Brunswick Windrush, five 100-gram (3.5-oz.) skeins dark rose #90583 (A), four skeins maroon #90024 (B), three skeins medium jade #90592 (C), two skeins light purple #90161 (D), one skein each winterberry #90872 (E) and light brown #90782 (F). Crochet hook size 10/J (6 mm) or size required to obtain gauge. Poplin-type cotton, 36" wide, ¾ yard each dark red and purple. Lightweight fabric for lining wall hanging, ⅞ yard. Matching sewing threads. Pellon Fusible Web. Pillow form, 12". Fabric for pillow, ⅜ yard.

GAUGE: 4 sc = 1"; 9 rows = 2".

Notes: When changing colors, work last sc of one color until there are 2 lps on hook; finish sc with new color. Work over strand of background color until it is needed again. Use separate balls of design color (small squares); do not carry these colors across work.

AFGHAN

SQUARE: With background color, ch 32.

Row 1: Following Chart 1 for placement of blocks of design color, sc in 2nd ch from hook and in each ch across—31 sc. Ch 1, turn.

Row 2: Following chart, sc in each sc. Ch 1, turn each row. Repeat row 2 to top of chart—39 rows. End off.

Square 1 (make six): Use C for background, D for design blocks.

Square 2 (make four): Use B for background, A for design blocks.

Square 3 (make two): Use E for background, B for design blocks.

STRIPS: Following Chart 2 for placement of squares on afghan, make three strips.

First Strip: With F, work 5 rows 31 sc across top of

Square 2, Square 1 and Square 3. With F, sew four squares tog to form strip at left of chart.

Second Strip: With F, work 5 rows of 31 sc across two Square 1's and one Square 2. With F, sew four squares tog to form center strip.

Third Strip: Work third strip in same way, following strip at right of chart.

Working along inner (right-hand) edge of first strip with F, work 5 rows of sc. Repeat on right-hand edge of center strip. Sew strip tog to form center of afghan.

BORDER: With A, ch 28.

Row 1: Sc in 2nd ch from hook and in each ch—27 sc. Ch 1, turn.

Row 2: Sc in each sc. Ch 1, turn. Repeat row 2 for required length. Make four borders (two to fit across top and bottom of afghan, two to fit along sides). Sew in place. With D, make four pieces 27 sc wide to fit the four corners. Sew in place.

EDGING: With C, work 2 rnds of sc around afghan, working 3 sc in each corner. Join; end off.

APPLIQUÉS: Cut twelve pieces each of dark red and purple fabric, 10″ × 4″. Cut out a triangle at each end of each piece as shown on pattern. Fold ½″ seam allowance to wrong side on long edges; press.

Fold edges of triangle to wrong side on fold lines; press. Secure seam allowance with fusible web or other iron-on adhesive to insure crisp edges. Machine-stitch around each piece ¹⁄₁₆″ in from edge. Center one piece at right angles to another piece of same color; machine-stitch pieces tog. Hand-sew appliqués to afghan squares, placing dark red appliqués straight on six Square 1's, purple appliqués on the diagonal on remaining six squares.

WALL HANGING

Following directions for afghan square, make two squares each of Square 1 and Square 2. With F, work 5 rows of 31 sc across top of a Square 1 and a Square 2. Sew each to bottom of opposite square to form two strips. With F, work 5 rows of sc along long inner edge of one strip. Sew to inner edge of second strip.

BORDER (make four): With B, ch 16.

Row 1: Sc in 2nd ch from hook and in each ch—15 sc. Ch 1, turn. Work even on 15 sc until piece is long enough to fit across side of wall hanging. With B, sew a border to top, bottom and sides of wall hang-

CHART 1

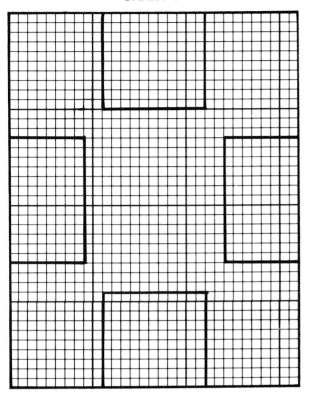

CHART 2

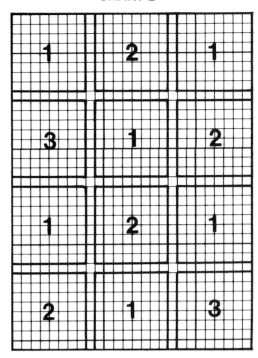

APPLIQUÉ PATTERN

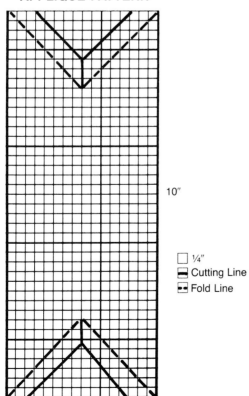

10″

4″

☐ ¼″
▣ Cutting Line
▣▣ Fold Line

ing. With D, make four pieces 15 sc wide to fit the four corners. Sew in place.

Edging: With C, work 2 rnds of sc around wall hanging, working 3 sc in each corner. Join; end off.

APPLIQUÉS: Cut four pieces each of dark red and purple fabric, 10″ × 4″. Finish appliqués as for afghan. Hand-sew appliqués to squares on the diagonal, dark red appliqués on Square 1, purple appliqués on Square 2.

FINISHING: Line back of wall hanging with fabric. Tack lining to wall hanging with long basting sts across top and bottom of squares.

PILLOW

Following directions for afghan square, make Square 3. With F, work 5 rnds of sc around square, working 3 sc in each corner each rnd. Join each rnd with sl st in first sc, ch 1. With C, work 1 rnd of sc around square.

APPLIQUÉ: Cut two pieces of dark red fabric, 10″ × 4″. Finish appliqué as for afghan. Hand-sew to pillow square on the diagonal.

FINISHING: Cut two pieces of pillow fabric, 13″ square. With right sides tog, stitch pieces tog on three sides, making ½″ seams. Turn pillow to right side, insert pillow form, close opening. Sew crocheted piece to pillow.

YOUNGSTERS' DELIGHTS

Crochet for children is most often thought of in terms of clothing, but clever and imaginative use of the technique can also produce fun projects for young people. Crocheting is relatively easy and the projects presented here can be used as bases for new ways to make games, toys, and other nontraditional crochet items. Older children can even turn out some of these projects with only minimal help from an adult. So, whether you use these ideas for inspiration for yourself or some young person you know, they're sure to be popular.

Old MacDonald and Friends

Crochet MacDonald and all his friends, and clothe him and Mrs. MacDonald with simple sewing to create an amusing play corner for youngsters.

BARN

SIZE: 11″ × 14″, 18½″ high.

MATERIALS: Coats & Clark Red Heart® 4-ply crochet yarn, Art. E. 267, four 100-gram (3.5-oz.) skeins vermilion #921 (A), two skeins blue #849 (B), one skein green #689 (C), small amount of yellow #261 (D) for embroidery. Crochet hook size 9/I (5.5 mm) or size required to obtain gauge. Green felt for lining, 1 yard. Three buttons ⅝″ in diameter. Seven 12″ × 18″ sheets of plastic canvas. Tapestry needle.

GAUGE: 13 sts = 4″; 4 rows = 1″.

BASE: With C, ch 35, having 13 ch sts to 4″.

Row 1: Sc in 2nd ch from hook and in each ch across—34 sc. Mark this row for right side of work. Ch 1, turn.

Row 2: Sc in each sc across—34 sc. Ch 1, turn. Repeat row 2 until total length is 14″, end with a row worked on right side. Fasten off.

SIDE SECTION (make two): With C, ch 35.

Row 1: Sc in 2nd ch from hook and in each ch across—34 sc. Mark this row for right side of work. Ch 1, turn.

Rows 2 and 3: Sc in each sc across. Ch 1, turn.

Row 4: Sc in each sc to last sc; draw up a lp in last sc, drop C; with A, yo and draw through both lps on hook—color change made. Fasten off C. Always change color in this way and fasten off dropped color. Ch 1, turn.

Rows 5–43: Sc in each sc across. Ch 1, turn. At end of row 43 make a color change to B. Ch 1, turn. Complete roof section as follows:

Rows 44–82: Repeat row 2. Fasten off.

BACK: With C, ch 47.

Row 1: Sc in 2nd ch from hook and in each ch across—46 sc. Mark this row for right side of work. Ch 1, turn.

Rows 2–4: Repeat rows 2–4 of side section.

Rows 5–42: Sc in each sc across. Ch 1, turn.

Row 43 (shape peak): Draw up a lp in each of next 2 sc, yo and draw through all lps on hook—dec made; sc in each sc across to last 2 sc, dec over last 2 sc. Ch 1, turn.

Next Row: Work even. Repeat last 2 rows once more. Then repeat row 43 until 2 sc remain. Fasten off.

FRONT: Work same as back.

HANDLE: With 2 strands of B held tog, ch 33.

Row 1: Sc in 2nd ch from hook and in each ch across—32 sc. Ch 1, turn.

Rows 2–4: Sc in each sc across. Ch 1, turn. Fasten off.

FINISHING: With D, embroider outline of barn door and window on front of barn with a chain stitch (see Embroidery Stitch Details, page 78). Having each piece of plastic canvas ⅛″ smaller on each side than crocheted barn sections, cut a piece of plastic canvas for each of the following: the lower part of each side section, for each upper part of a side section, one piece each for front section, back section and base. Cut a piece of green felt the same size as each piece of plastic canvas. With yarn, tack the plastic canvas to wrong side of each barn section. Place felt over plastic canvas and sew in place. Sew side sections to corresponding narrow edges of base; sew front and back to corresponding long edges of base, making sure that all right sides are to the outside and all marked rows are down. Sew corresponding side edges of the four parts together to form the barn. Sew the corresponding rows 42–56 of the roof and peak sections together at each upper corner of barn.

Roof Trim for Front Section: With B make a chain to measure the length of outer edges of the peaked section of the front of the barn, then sl st in each ch across. Fasten off. Sew trim in place on peak. Make roof trim for back of barn in same way.

Button loop (make three): With B, ch 8. Fasten off, leaving a 10″ end for sewing. Sew button loops evenly spaced to edge of one B section of roof. Sew buttons to opposite roof section to correspond. Sew one end of handle to peak of front roof and other end to peak of back roof.

PIG

SIZE: About 5″ high.

MATERIALS: Coats & Clark Red Heart® 4-ply crochet yarn, Art. E. 267, one 100-gram (3.5-oz.) skein pale rose #755. Crochet hook size 8/H (5 mm) or size required to obtain gauge. Piece of black felt, 1″ square for eyes. Piece of pink felt, 4″ square for ears. Black embroidery floss. Polyester stuffing.

GAUGE: 4 sts = 1″; 4 rnds = 1″.

BODY: Beg at snout, ch 3. Join with sl st to form ring.

Rnd 1: Ch 1, 6 sc in ring; do not join rnds but carry a contrasting color thread up between last and first sc to indicate beg of rnds.

Rnd 2: 2 sc in each sc around—12 sc.

Rnd 3: (Sc in next 2 sc; 2 sc in next sc—inc made) 4 times—16 sc.

Rnds 4–8: Sc in each sc around.

Rnd 9: (Sc in next sc, inc in next sc) 8 times—24 sc.

Rnd 10: (Sc in next 3 sc, inc in next sc) 6 times—30 sc.

Rnd 11: (Sc in next 4 sc, inc in next sc) 6 times—36 sc.

Rnd 12: (Sc in next 4 sc, inc in next sc) 7 times; sc in last sc—43 sc.

Rnds 13 and 14: Sc in each sc around.

Rnd 15: (Sc in next 2 sc; draw up a lp in each of next 2 sc, yo and draw through all lps on hook—dec made) 3 times; with a safety pin, mark last dec made for lower section of head, (sc in next 2 sc, dec over next 2 sc) twice; sc in each remaining sc around—38 sc.

Rnds 16 and 17: Sc in each sc around.

Rnd 18: Sc in next 2 sc, (inc in next sc, sc in next 3 sc) 3 times; inc in next sc, sc in next 2 sc, inc in next sc, (sc in next 3 sc, inc in next sc) 5 times—48 sc.

Rnds 19–26: Sc in each sc around.

Rnd 27: Dec 6 sc evenly spaced, sc in each sc around.

Rnds 28–30: Stuffing as work progresses, repeat rnd 27, being careful decs do not fall directly over decs of previous rnd. Remove marker and shape back section as follows: * Sc in next 2 sc, dec over next 2 sc, repeat from * around until opening is ½" in diameter. Join with sl st in next st. Leaving a 10" end, cut yarn and draw through remaining sts, pull together to close and secure.

LEG (make four): Work as for body until rnd 2 is completed—12 sc.

Rnds 3–6: Sc in each sc around. Fasten off, leaving a 12" end for sewing. Stuff. With pin marker at front of lower section of head, sew last rnd of each leg to lower section, having the front legs about 3" in from beg of snout and 1½" apart; sew hind legs about 1¼" from back end and ½" apart.

TAIL: Ch 16 to measure 3", sl st in 2nd ch from hook and in each ch across. Fasten off, leaving a length for sewing. Sew in place. Tie a knot at free end.

Following pattern, cut out pink felt ears. Holding two pieces together and leaving front edge open, sew remaining outer edges together with overcast stitches. Make a pleat on straight edge, with ears about 1½" apart; sew pleated edge to top of body as shown.

From black felt cut two circles each ½" in diameter for eyes. Glue or tack in place as shown.

With black floss, embroider straight stitches for nostrils on snout as shown.

SHEEP

SIZE: About 9½" tall.

MATERIALS: Coats & Clark Red Heart® 4-ply crochet yarn, Art. E. 267, one 100-gram (3.5-oz.) skein pale rose #755. Crochet hook size 8/H (5 mm) or size required to obtain gauge. Piece of brown felt, 6" square, for legs and ears. Piece of black felt, 3" square, for eyes, nose, and feet. Polyester stuffing.

GAUGE: 4 sts = 1"; 4 rnds = 1".

HEAD: Beg at front, ch 3. Join with sl st to form ring.

Rnd 1: Ch 1, 6 sc in ring; do not join rnds but carry a contrasting color thread up between last and first sc on each rnd to indicate beg of rnds.

Rnd 2: (2 sc in next sc—inc made; sc in next sc, inc in next sc) twice—10 sc.

Rnds 3 and 4: Sc in each sc around.

Rnd 5: (Sc in next 2 sc, inc in next sc) 3 times; sc in next sc—13 sc.

Rnd 6: (Inc in next sc, sc in next sc) 6 times; inc in next sc—20 sc.

Rnds 7–11: Sc in each sc around, stuffing firmly as work progresses.

Rnd 12: (Sc in next 2 sc; draw up a lp in next 2 sc, yo and draw through all lps on hook—dec made) 5 times—15 sc.

Rnd 13: (Sc in next sc, dec over next 2 sc) 5 times—10 sc. Sl st in next sc. Leaving a 10" end, cut yarn and draw end through remaining sts, pull together and secure.

NECK AND BODY: Beg at top of neck, ch 10. Join with sl st to form ring.

Rnd 1: Ch 1, sc in joining and in each ch around—10 sc; do not join rnds but carry up a thread as before.

Rnd 2: Sc in each sc around.

Rnd 3: Sc in next 9 sc, inc in next sc—11 sc.

Rnd 4: Inc in next sc, sc in next 10 sc—12 sc.

Rnd 5: Ch 4, sc in 2nd ch from hook, sc in next 2 ch, sc in next 12 sc; working along opposite side of ch-4, sc in next 2 ch, make 3 sc in next ch—20 sc. Remove contrasting color thread and place this thread between last st worked and next st to indicate beg of rnd.

Rnd 6: Sc in each sc around.

PATTERN FOR PIG'S EAR (Actual Size)

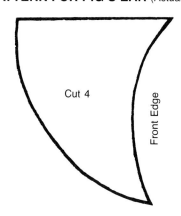

Cut 4

Front Edge

Rnd 7: Ch 7, sc in 2nd ch from hook, sc in next 5 ch, sc in next 20 sc, working along opposite side of ch 7, sc in next 5 ch, make 3 sc in next ch—34 sc; remove thread and place it between last st worked and next st as before.

Rnds 8–16: Sc in each sc around. Shape underside of body as follows: * Sc in next 2 sc, dec over next 2 sc, repeat from * until 14 sc remain, sl st in next sc. Cut yarn, leaving a 10″ end for sewing. Stuff neck and body firmly and sew underside seam. With front of head facing forward, sew head to top of neck.

UPPER LEG (make four): Starting at lower edge, ch 5. Join with sl st to form ring.

Rnd 1: Ch 1, 9 sc in ring; do not join rnds but carry up a thread as before.

Rnds 2–4: Sc in each sc around. Cut yarn, leaving an 8″ end for sewing. Do not stuff. Holding work flat, sew upper edge closed. Sew upper legs in place as shown.

LOWER LEG (make four): Cut a piece of brown felt 2″ × 3″; starting at the 2″ edge, roll felt tightly. Sew other 2″ edge to the roll. Cut a piece of black felt ⅜″ × 1½″ and sew around one end of lower leg to form hoof. Insert lower leg ½″ into opening of upper leg and sew securely.

TAIL: Row 1: Ch 11, sc in 2nd ch from hook and in each ch across—10 sc. Turn.

Row 2: Sl st in each sc across. Cut yarn, leaving an 8″ end for sewing. Sew in place.

FLEECE: Loosely make a chain about 5 yards long and wind into a ball. Leaving the first 6 rnds on head and the underside on body free and making small loops, sew chain to head, body and upper legs as shown. If needed, make more loose chain.

Using patterns, cut eyes from black felt and ears from brown felt; glue or tack in place as shown. Cut a ⅜″ × ⅜″ piece of black felt for nose and glue or tack in place.

PATTERNS FOR SHEEP (Actual Size)

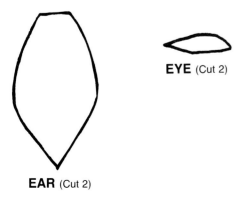

EYE (Cut 2)

EAR (Cut 2)

Cow

SIZE: About 12½″ high.

MATERIALS: Coats & Clark Red Heart® 4-ply crochet yarn, Art. E. 267, one 100-gram (3.5-oz.) skein off-white #3 (A), small amount bronze #286 (B). Crochet hook size 9/I (5.5 mm) or size required to obtain gauge. Tapestry needle. Scraps of black, tan, and pink felt. Polyester stuffing.

GAUGE: 7 sc = 2″; 7 rnds = 2″.

Note: Head and body are worked in one piece.

HEAD AND BODY: Beg at top of head with A, ch 4.

Rnd 1: Sc in 2nd ch from hook and in next ch, 3 sc in last ch; working along opposite side of starting chain sc in next ch, make 2 sc in next ch—8 sc. Do not join rnds but carry a contrasting color thread up between last and first sc to indicate beg of rnds.

Rnd 2: Sc in next 3 sc, 3 sc in next sc, sc in next 3 sc, 3 sc in last sc—12 sc.

Rnd 3: Sc in next 4 sc, 3 sc in next sc, sc in next 5 sc, 3 sc in next sc, sc in last sc—16 sc.

Rnd 4: Sc in 4 sc, 2 sc in next sc, 3 sc in next sc, 2 sc in next sc, sc in 5 sc, 2 sc in next sc, 3 sc in next sc, 2 sc in next sc, sc in last sc—24 sc.

Rnd 5: Sc in 6 sc, 2 sc in next sc, 3 sc in next sc, 2 sc in next sc, sc in 9 sc, 2 sc in next sc, 3 sc in next sc, 2 sc in next sc, sc in last 3 sc—32 sc.

Rnd 6: Sc in 8 sc, 2 sc in next sc, 3 sc in next sc, 2 sc in next sc, sc in next 13 sc, 2 sc in next sc, 3 sc in next sc, 2 sc in next sc, sc in last 5 sc—40 sc.

Rnds 7–9: Sc in each sc around. Mark 9th st before end of rnd 9. Remove thread marker. Cut yarn and fasten off end. Now establish upper back section on next 2 rnds as follows:

Rnd 10: Join A in marked st, ch 7, sc in 2nd ch from hook and in next 5 ch; working around head and body section in next 19 sc, 3 sc in next sc, sc in next 19 sc; working along opposite side of chain, sc in next 6 ch—53 sc.

Rnd 11: Ch 18, sc in 2nd ch from hook and in next 16 ch, sc in 26 sc; 3 sc in next sc, sc in next 26 sc; working along opposite side of chain, sc in 17 ch—89 sc. Place a thread marker to indicate beg of rnd as before.

Rnd 12: 2 sc in next sc, sc in each sc to center sc of the 3-sc group on previous rnd, 3 sc in center sc, sc in each sc to last sc, 2 sc in last sc—93 sc.

Rnds 13–16: Sc in each sc around.

Rnd 17: Sc in 44 sc; draw up a lp in each of next 2 sc, yo and draw through all 3 lps on hook—dec made; sc in next sc for center st on nose section, dec over next 2 sc, sc in 44 sc—91 sc.

Rnd 18: Sc in each sc around.

Rnd 19: Sc in 43 sc, dec over next 2 sc, sc in next sc, dec over next 2 sc, sc in 43 sc—89 sc.

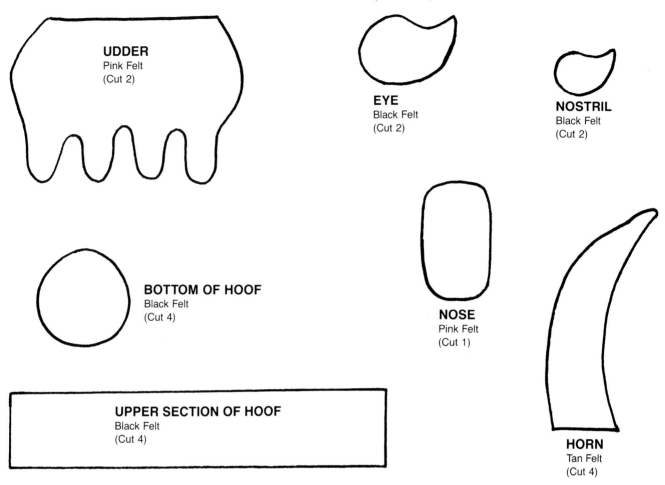

PATTERNS FOR COW (Actual Size)

UDDER
Pink Felt
(Cut 2)

EYE
Black Felt
(Cut 2)

NOSTRIL
Black Felt
(Cut 2)

BOTTOM OF HOOF
Black Felt
(Cut 4)

NOSE
Pink Felt
(Cut 1)

UPPER SECTION OF HOOF
Black Felt
(Cut 4)

HORN
Tan Felt
(Cut 4)

Rnd 20: Sc in 41 sc, sk next 7 sc, sc in next 41 sc—82 sc.

Rnd 21: Sc in 37 sc, sk next 8 sc, sc in next 37 sc—74 sc.

Rnd 22: Sc in each sc around.

Rnds 23–24: Sc in first sc, dec over next 2 sc, sc in each sc around to last 2 sc, dec over last 2 sc. There are 70 sts on last rnd.

Rnds 25 and 26: Sc in each sc around.

Rnd 27: Sc in 34 sc, dec over next 2 sc, sc in 34 sc—69 sc.

Rnd 28: Sc in 31 sc, sk next 7 sc, sc in 31 sc—62 sc.

Rnd 29: * Sc in next 3 sc, dec over next 2 sc. Repeat from * around to last sc, sc in last sc—49 sc.

Rnd 30: Sc in next sc, * dec over next 2 sc, sc in next 3 sc. Repeat from * around, end last repeat, sc in last sc—39 sc.

Rnd 31: Sc in next sc, * dec over next 2 sc, sc in next 3 sc. Repeat from * around, end last repeat with sc in last sc—31 sc. Drop lp from hook to be picked up later.

Embroider cow's body as follows: With tapestry needle and B, embroider four spots on each side of cow as shown by making slanted diagonal stitches over each sc in the area of the spot. Continue to work in rnds on lower opening as follows: **Next Rnd:** Pick up dropped lp; sc in next sc, * dec over next 2 sc, sc in next 2 sc. Repeat from * around, end with dec over last 2 sc.

Last Rnd: Dec over next 2 sc, * sc in next sc, dec over next 2 sc. Repeat from * around; sl st in next sc. Cut yarn leaving a 10″ end for sewing. Stuff body and sew all openings closed.

FRONT LEG (make two): Beg at hoof end with A, ch 10. Join with sl st to form ring.

Rnd 1: Ch 1, sc in joining and in each sc around—10 sc; do not join rnds but carry a thread up as before.

Rnds 2–8: Sc in each sc around.

Rnd 9: Sc in next 3 sc, (2 sc in next sc, sc in next 2 sc) twice; 2 sc in last sc—13 sc.

Rnds 10–16: Sc in each sc around. Cut yarn, leaving a 10″ end for sewing. Stuff leg firmly. Sew last rnd of each leg to body as shown.

HIND LEG (make two): Work as for front leg until rnd 8 is completed.

Rnd 9: (2 sc in next sc, sc in next sc) twice; 2 sc in each of next 2 sc, (sc in next sc, 2 sc in next sc) twice—16 sc.

Rnds 10–18: Sc in sc around. Cut yarn, leaving a 10″ end for sewing. Stuff leg firmly. Sew each leg in place as shown.

EAR (make two): With B, ch 9.

Rnd 1: Sc in 2nd ch from hook, dc in each of next 6 ch, 3 sc in last ch; working along opposite side of starting chain, sc in next 6 ch, 3 sc in next ch; do not join.

Rnd 2: Sc in next sc, sc in next 6 dc, sc in next sc, sl st in next sc; do not work over remaining sts. Cut yarn, leaving an 8″ end for sewing. Sew ears in place as shown, having right side of work facing forward front of head.

HOOF (make four): From black felt, cut lower and upper hoof pieces, using the actual-size patterns. Sew narrow ends of one upper hoof section together to form a ring; then sew a round lower hoof piece in place to one open end of ring. Push hoof in place on end of leg and sew in place as shown.

TAIL: With B, ch 23.

Row 1: Sl st in 2nd ch from hook and in each ch across. Fasten off. Cut 4 strands of B each 5″ long; fold in half to form a loop and draw loop through end of tail to form a tuft. Trim ends to 1″. Sew tail in place.

UDDER: Following pattern, from pink felt cut udder pieces. Sew pieces together, leaving straight edge open. Stuff, then sew to underbody by sewing around open edges of udder.

HORN (make two): Following pattern, from tan felt cut horns. Holding two pieces together, sew around outer edge, leaving the straight narrow end open. Stuff firmly and sew in place on head. Following patterns, cut nose, eyes and nostrils. Sew nose to front of head and sew nostrils in place. Sew on eyes.

FARMER AND WIFE

SIZE: Farmer is 16″ tall; his wife is 14″ tall.

MATERIALS: Coats & Clark Red Heart® 4-ply crochet yarn, Art. E. 267. For farmer, 2 oz. vermilion #921 (A), 1 oz. each coral #246 (B), brown #360 (C), yellow #261 (D), light gold #603 (E). For wife, 2 oz. blue #818 (F), 1 oz. each coral #246 (B), brown #360 (C), black #12 (G), white #1 (H). Crochet hook size 8/H (5 mm) or size required to obtain gauge. For farmer, a piece of blue denim 10″ × 20″. Two buttons ⅜″ in diameter. For wife, a 4″ length of white pregathered eyelet lace 5½″ wide; 14″ of white pre-gathered eyelet lace 1½″ wide; 27″ of red grosgrain ribbon ⅜″ wide. For farmer and wife, scraps of blue felt for eyes and red felt for mouths. Polyester stuffing.

GAUGE: 4 sc = 1″; 4 rnds = 1″.

FARMER

HEAD: Beg at neck with B, ch 2.

Rnd 1: 6 sc in 2nd ch from hook; do not join rnds but carry a contrasting color thread up between last and first sc on each rnd to indicate beg of rnds.

Rnd 2: 2 sc in each sc around—12 sc.

Rnd 3: (Sc in next sc; 2 sc in next sc—inc made) 6 times—18 sc.

Rnd 4: (Sc in next 2 sc, inc in next sc) 6 times—24 sc.

Rnd 5: (Sc in next 3 sc, inc in next sc) 6 times—30 sc.

Rnd 6: Increasing 4 sc evenly spaced, sc in each sc around—34 sc.

Rnds 7–14: Sc in each sc around.

Shape top of head as follows: * Sc in next 2 sc; draw up a lp in each of next 2 sc, yo and draw through all lps on hook—dec made. Repeat from * until opening is ½″ in diameter, stuffing head firmly as work progresses. Leaving a 10″ end, cut yarn and draw end through remaining sts; pull sts together to close opening; secure end.

BODY: Beg at neck with A, work as for head until rnd 4 is completed.

Rnd 5: Increasing 4 sc evenly spaced, sc in each sc around—28 sc.

Rnds 6–18: Sc in each sc around.

Rnd 19: Decreasing 4 sts evenly spaced, sc in each sc around—24 sc. Do not cut yarn. Mark 13th sc from beg of rnd with a safety pin.

FIRST LEG: Ch 3, join with sl st to sc marked with a safety pin. Ch 1, turn.

Rnd 1: With right side facing, sc in marked sc, sc in next 11 sc, sc in next 3 ch sts—15 sc. Remove safety pin. Do not join rnds but carry up a thread as before.

Rnds 2–18: Sc in each sc around.

Rnd 19: Decreasing 3 sts evenly spaced, sc in each sc around—12 sc.

Rnds 20–22: Sc in each sc around. Fasten off, leaving a 10″ end and close as before. Stuff leg and body firmly.

SECOND LEG: With right side facing, join A to opposite side of first ch st on previous leg.

Rnd 1: Ch 1, sc in joining, sc in opposite side of next 2 ch sts, sc in each remaining sc on body—15 sc; do not join rnds but carry up a thread as before. Stuff leg firmly as work progresses and complete as for first leg.

ARM (make two): Beg at hand end with B, work as for head until rnd 2 is completed—12 sc.

Rnds 3 and 4: Sc in each sc around.

Rnd 5: Sc in first sc, dec over next 2 sc, sc in next 4 sc, dec over next 2 sc, sc in each sc to last sc, draw up a lp in last sc, drop B; with A, yo and draw

PATTERN FOR OVERALLS

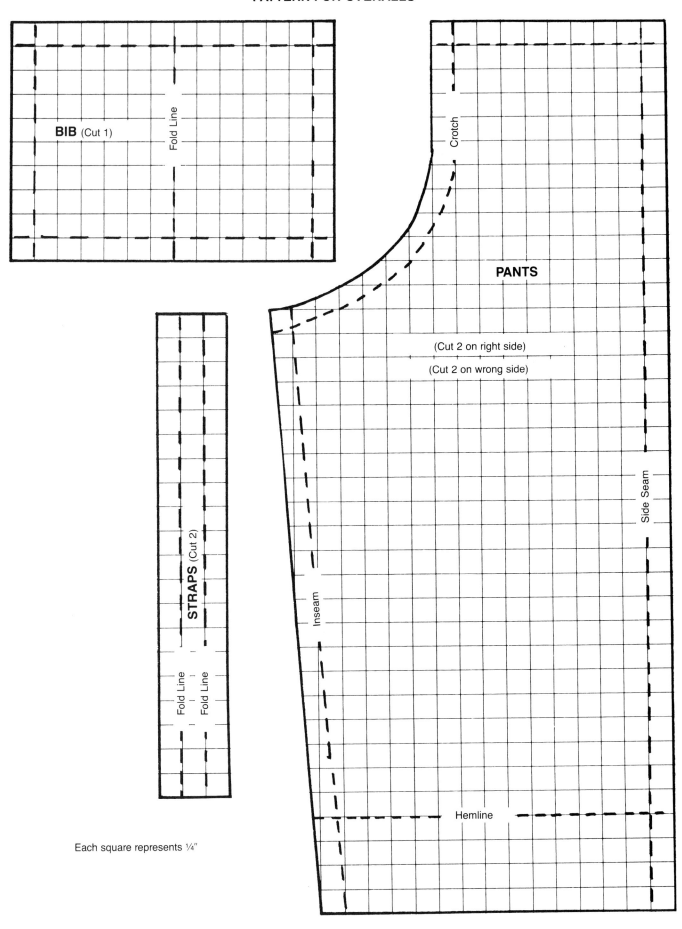

BIB (Cut 1)

Fold Line

Crotch

PANTS

(Cut 2 on right side)

(Cut 2 on wrong side)

STRAPS (Cut 2)

Fold Line

Fold Line

Inseam

Side Seam

Hemline

Each square represents ¼"

through the 2 lps on hook, fasten off B—color change made—10 sc. Always change color in this way and fasten off color not in use.

Rnds 6–10: Sc in each sc around.

Rnd 11: Increasing 2 sc evenly spaced, sc in each sc around—12 sc.

Rnds 12–14: Sc in each sc around.

Rnd 15: Work as for rnd 11—14 sc.

Rnds 16–20: Sc in each sc around. Fasten off, leaving a 10″ end. Stuff arm firmly and close as before. Sew head and arms to body as shown.

SHOE (make two): With E ch 8.

Row 1: Sc in 2nd ch from hook and in each ch across—7 sc. Ch 1, turn.

Rows 2–10: Sc in each sc across. Ch 1, turn. At end of last row fasten off. Fold piece in half, having row 1 and row 10 together; sew the 3 open edges together, stuffing shoe before closing. Work a row of sl sts along sewn and fold edges to form edge of sole.

HAT: Beg at crown with D, work as for head until rnd 5 is completed—30 sc.

Rnds 6–8: Sc in each sc around.

Rnd 9: (Sc in next 9 sc, inc in next sc) 3 times—33 sc.

Rnd 10: (Sc in next 2 sc, inc in next sc) 11 times—44 sc.

Rnd 11: (Sc in next 4 sc, inc in next sc) 8 times; sc in last 4 sc—52 sc.

Rnd 12: (Sc in next 5 sc, inc in next sc) 8 times; sc in last 4 sc—60 sc.

Rnd 13: Sl st in each sc around. Fasten off. With a double strand of B and a yarn needle, sew around base of crown with long running stitches for hat band; tie ends.

HAIR: With a double strand of C threaded in a yarn needle and using long straight stitches, work back and forth from center crown to hairline on face as shown.

Sew hat in place on head.

From blue felt cut 2 round pieces each ½″ in diameter for eyes. From red felt cut a small crescent shape for mouth. Glue or tack eyes and mouth in place.

Sew a shoe to each leg, having end of leg at top on back end of shoe and being careful to have shoe face forward. Lace a 10″ length of D back and forth over instep on top of shoe to make a lace; tie ends into bow as shown.

NECK TRIM: With A make a chain 3½″ long; cut yarn, leaving a 5″ end for sewing. Place chain around neck and sew ends together.

OVERALLS: Pin pattern pieces for overalls onto denim and cut out. Sew side seams, crotch seams and inseam. Fold legs on hemline and sew in place. Turn under ¼″ at waist and press. With right sides together, fold bib on fold line; sew side seams. Turn right side out and press. Place lower edge of bib behind waist on pants, centering on front crotch seam, and baste. Topstitch ⅛″ from folded edge on waist. Fold straps along fold lines; press and stitch along center. Tack in place at top edge of bib. Sew buttons in place on bib as shown. Put overalls on farmer, cross straps in back and tack in place, adjusting length.

WIFE

HEAD: Work as for head on farmer until rnd 5 is completed—30 sc.

Rnd 6: Inc in next sc, sc in each sc around—31 sc.

Rnds 7–13: Sc in each sc around. Now shape top of head and complete head same as for farmer.

BODY: With F, work as for body on farmer.

FIRST LEG: Work as for first leg on farmer until rnd 3 is completed, changing to H at end of last rnd—15 sc.

Rnd 4: Decreasing 2 sts evenly spaced, sc in each sc around—13 sc.

Rnds 5–15: Sc in each sc around. Fasten off and close as before. Stuff leg and body firmly.

SECOND LEG: With F, work as for second leg on farmer until rnd 3 is completed, changing to H at end of last rnd—1 sc. Starting with rnd 4, complete as for first leg for wife, stuffing leg as work progresses.

ARM (make two): Work as for arm on farmer until rnd 1 is completed—6 sc.

Rnd 2: (Sc in next sc, inc in next sc) 3 times—9 sc.

Rnd 3: Sc in each sc around.

Rnd 4: Dec over next 2 sc, sc in each sc around, changing to F at end of rnd—8 scs.

Rnds 5–10: Sc in each sc around.

Rnd 11: Increasing 2 sc evenly spaced, sc in each sc around—10 sc.

Rnds 12–18: Sc in each sc around. Fasten off, leaving a 10″ end. Stuff and close as before. Sew head and arms to body as shown.

SHOES (make two): With G, ch 7.

Row 1: Sc in 2nd ch from hook and in each ch across—6 sc. Ch 1, turn. Complete as for farmer.

SKIRT: Beg on a side edge of skirt with F, ch 19, having 4 ch sts to 1″.

Row 1: Sc in 2nd ch from hook and in each ch across—18 sc. Ch 1, turn.

Rows 2–48: Sc in each sc across. Ch 1, turn. At end of last row, ch 1; do not turn.

Lower Border on Skirt: Row 1: Working along next long edge, sc in end st of each row. Ch 1, turn.

Row 2: Sc in each sc across. Fasten off. Sew side edges of skirt together. Gathering top edge to fit, sew skirt to body at waist.

HAIR: With C, embroider hair on head as for

farmer. To make topknot on head, cut twelve 8" strands of yarn. Tie a piece of yarn around strands at each end to secure; twist and then coil to form a topknot; sew in place on crown of head, tucking ends under.

Cut eyes and mouth same as for farmer and glue or tack in place.

Sew on shoes as for farmer.

NECK TRIM: With F, work same as for farmer.

APRON: Turn under and hem the raw edges on the 5½"-wide piece of eyelet lace. Center grosgrain ribbon along pregathered edge of lace, leaving an end for a tie at either side; sew in place. Tie apron around waist and tie a bow in back. Cut the 14" strip of 1½"-wide lace in half; place over shoulders on wife, crossing in front and back. Tuck ends in behind apron and ribbon and tack in place; trim ends.

ROOSTER

SIZE: About 5½" high.

MATERIALS: Coats & Clark Red Heart® 4-ply crochet yarn, Art. E. 267, one ounce of #283 brown (A), ½ ounce of #603 light gold (B), and a few yards of #286 bronze (C). Crochet hook size 9/I (5.5 mm) or size required to obtain gauge. Scraps of red, yellow, black, and white felt. Polyester stuffing.

GAUGE: 7 sts = 2"; 7 rnds = 2".

HEAD AND BODY: Starting at top of head with B, ch 3. Join with sl st to form ring.

Rnd 1: Ch 1, 5 sc in ring; do not join rnds but carry a contrasting color thread up between last and first sc to indicate beg of rnds.

PATTERNS FOR ROOSTER
Each square represents ¼"

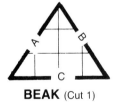

BEAK (Cut 1)

FOOT (Cut 2)

WATTLE (Cut 2)

COMB (Cut 1)

Rnd 2: (2 sc in next sc—inc made) twice; 3 sc in next sc; (inc in next sc) twice—11 sc.

Rnd 3: Sc in each sc around.

Rnd 4: Inc in next sc, sc in next 4 sc, inc in next sc, sc in next 5 sc—13 sc.

Rnds 5 and 6: Sc in each sc around.

Rnd 7: (Inc in next sc) twice; sc in next 5 sc, inc in next sc, sc in next 5 sc—16 sc.

Rnd 8: Sc in next 15 sc; draw up a lp in last sc, drop B; with A, yo and draw through the 2 lps on hook—color change made. Fasten off B.

Rnd 9: Sl st in next sc, remove thread marker, ch 4 for start of back shaping, 3 sc in 2nd ch from hook, sc in next 2 ch, sc in next 6 sc, (inc in next sc) 3 times; sc in next 6 sc, working along opposite side of chain sc in next 3 ch—26 sc.

Rnd 10: Sc in 26 sc.

Rnd 11: Sl st in next sc, ch 2, sc in 2nd ch from hook, sc in next 25 sc; working along opposite side of chain, inc in next ch—28 sc. Place a thread marker between last st worked and next st as before.

Rnd 12: Sc in next 11 sc, (inc in next sc, sc in next sc) twice; inc in next sc, sc in next 10 sc, inc in next sc, sc in next sc.

Rnds 13 and 14: Sc in each sc around.

Rnd 15: Sc in next 15 sc, (draw up a lp in next 2 sc, yo and draw through all 3 lps on hook—dec made) twice; sc in next 13 sc—30 sc.

Rnds 16–17: Sc in each sc around. Shape underside as follows: * Sc in next 2 sc, dec over next 2 sc. Repeat from * until opening is 1½" in diameter. Leaving a 10" end for sewing, cut yarn. Stuff firmly and sew opening closed. With B and alternating long and short stitches, embroider around neck as shown.

WING (make two): With A, ch 11.

Row 1: Sc in 2nd ch from hook, mark this st for wing tip, sc in each ch across—10 sc. Ch 1, turn.

Row 2: Sc in first 9 sc; do not work in last st. Ch 1, turn.

Row 3: Sc in 9 sc. Ch 1, turn.

Row 4: Sc in first 8 sc. Fasten off. With C and alternating long and short straight stitches, embroider wing as shown. Sew in place, leaving wing tips free.

TAIL FEATHERS: With A, ch 12.

Row 1: Sc in 2nd ch from hook and in next 3 ch, dc in next 6 ch, sc in next ch. Ch 14, turn.

Row 2: Sc in 2nd ch from hook and in next 3 ch, dc in next 7 ch, sc in next ch; do not work in last ch. Ch 15, turn.

Row 4: Sc in 2nd ch from hook and in next 3 ch, dc in next 8 ch, sc in next ch; do not work in last ch. Cut yarn, leaving an 8" end for sewing. Slightly overlap and sew in place as shown.

LEG AND FOOT (make two): Cut a piece of yellow felt ½″ × 1″. Starting at ½″ edge roll piece up tightly to make leg, then sew the ½″ edge in place to keep from rolling. Using pattern, cut two feet from yellow felt and sew to ends of legs. Sew legs in place.

EYE (make two): Cut a round piece from white felt ⅜″ in diameter and a ¼″ round piece from black felt. Glue black felt on top of white felt. Glue eyes in place.

BEAK: Using pattern, cut beak from yellow felt. Sew shorter edges A and B together; then sew longer edge C to head. Using patterns, cut wattles and comb from red felt. Tack in place as shown.

Goose

SIZE: About 5¾″ tall.

MATERIALS: Coats & Clark Red Heart® 4-ply crochet yarn, Art. E. 267, one ounce of #1 white. Crochet hook size 8/H (5 mm) or size required to obtain gauge. 4″ × 6″ piece of orange felt for beak, feet and legs; scraps of green felt for eyes. Polyester stuffing.

GAUGE: 4 sts = 1″; 4 rnds = 1″.

HEAD SECTION: Starting at top, ch 3. Join with sl st to form ring.

Rnd 1: Ch 1, 6 sc in ring; do not join rnds but carry a contrasting color thread up between last and first sc to indicate beg of rnds.

Rnd 2: 2 sc in next sc—inc made; inc in next 5 sc—12 sc.

Rnd 3: Sc in each sc around, ch 3 for beak extension; transfer thread marker between last ch and next sc and carry up as before.

Rnd 4: Sc in 2nd ch from hook, sc in next ch, sc in next 12 sc, sc in opposite side of next 2 ch of beak, 3 sc in next ch—19 sc.

Rnd 5: Sc in next 16 sc; do not work over remaining 3 sc.

Rnd 6: Sk the 3 sc not worked on previous rnd; draw up a lp in next 2 sc, yo and draw through all lps on hook—dec made at beg of rnd; sc in next sc, dec over last 2 sc—14 sc.

Rnd 7: Dec over first 2 sc, (sc in next 4 sc, dec over next 2 sc) twice—11 sc.

Rnds 8–11: Sc in each sc around, stuffing as work progresses.

Rnd 12: Sc in next sc, inc in next sc, sc in next 4 sc, (inc in next sc) twice; sc in last 3 sc—14 sc.

Rnd 13: Sc in next 8 sc, inc in next sc, sc in next sc, ch 5 for back extension; do not work over last 3 sc.

BODY SECTION: Transfer marker between last ch and next ch and carry up as before.

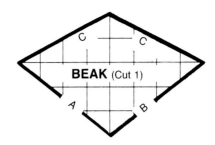

BEAK (Cut 1)

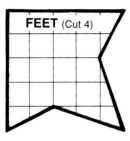

FEET (Cut 4)

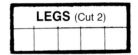

LEGS (Cut 2)

Rnd 1: Sc in 2nd ch from hook and in next 3 ch, sc in next sc, inc in next sc, sc in next 13 sc, sc in opposite side of next 4 ch, 3 sc in next ch—27 sc.

Rnd 2: Sc in next 24 sc, inc in next sc, sc in next sc, inc in last sc—29 sc.

Rnd 3: Sc in each sc around.

Rnd 4: Sc in next 28 sc, ch 4 for tail extension; do not work in last sc; transfer marker between last and next sc and carry up as before.

Rnd 5: Sc in 2nd ch from hook and in next 2 ch, sc in next 29 sc, sc in opposite side of next 3 ch, 3 sc in next ch—38 sc.

Rnd 6: Dec over next 2 sc, sc in next 14 sc; draw up a lp in next 3 sc, yo and draw through all lps on hook—2 sc dec made over 3 sc; sc in next 14 sc, dec over next 2 sc; do not work over last 3 sc—31 sc.

Rnd 7: Sk the 3 sc not worked on previous rnd; dec 2 sc over next 3 sc, sc in next 10 sc, dec over next 2 sc, sc in next sc, dec over next 2 sc, sc in next 10 sc, dec 2 sc over last 3 sc.

Rnd 8: Dec 2 sc over next 3 sc, sc in next 7 sc, dec over next 2 sc, sc in next sc, dec over next 2 sc, sc in next 7 sc, dec 2 sc over last 3 sc.

Rnd 9: Dec 2 sc over next 3 sc, sc in next 4 sc, dec

over next 2 sc, sc in next sc, dec over next 2 sc, sc in next 4 sc, dec 2 sc over last 3 sc. Cut yarn, leaving a 12″ length for sewing. Stuff firmly. Sew opening closed.

WING (make two): Starting at top edge, ch 9.

Row 1: Sc in 2nd ch from hook and in each ch across—8 sc. Mark beg of row for tip. Ch 1, turn.

Row 2: Sc in first 7 sc; do not work in last sc. Ch 1, turn.

Row 3: Sk first sc, sc in next 6 sc. Cut yarn, leaving an end for sewing. Leaving tip end free, sew opposite end of a wing to a side of body as shown.

Following pattern, from orange felt cut beak, legs and feet. Folding beak in half, sew edge A to edge B; place open end over beak on head and sew edge C to head. Holding two sections of each foot together, sew all edges together. Starting at narrow edge of leg section, roll tightly and tack down to secure. Sew a leg to center of a foot and then sew legs to body.

Using green felt, cut two circles each ⅜″ in diameter for eyes; glue or tack in place as shown.

Lamb

SIZE: About 6″ high.
MATERIALS: Coats & Clark Red Heart® 4-ply crochet yarn, Art. E. 267, one ounce of #1 white. Crochet hook size 9/I (5.5 mm) or size required to obtain gauge. Scraps of black, pink, and blue felt. Polyester stuffing.
GAUGE: 4 sts = 1″; 4 rnds = 1″.
HEAD: Starting at end of nose, ch 3. Join with sl st to form ring.

Rnd 1: Ch 1, 5 sc in ring; do not join rnds but carry a contrasting color thread up between last and first sc to indicate beg of rnds.

Rnd 2: (2 sc in next sc—inc made; sc in next sc) twice; inc in next sc—8 sc.

Rnd 3: Sc in each sc around.

Rnd 4: (Sc in next sc, inc in next sc) 3 times; sc in next 2 sc—11 sc.

Rnd 5: (Sc in next sc, inc in next sc) 5 times; sc in next sc—16 sc.

Rnds 6–8: Sc in each sc around.

Rnd 9: (Sc in next 2 sc; draw up a lp in each of next 2 sc, yo and draw through all 3 lps on hook—dec made) 4 times—12 sc.

Rnd 10: (Sc in next sc, dec over next 2 sc) 4 times—8 sc. Stuff head firmly. Leaving an 8″ end for sewing, cut yarn and draw end through sts of last rnd; pull tog and secure.

BODY: Beg at neck edge, ch 7. Join with sl st to form ring.

Rnd 1: Ch 1, sc in joining and in each ch around—8

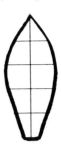

sc; do not join rnds but carry up a thread as before.

Rnd 2: Sc in each sc around.

Rnd 3: Form back section as follows: Ch 8, sc in 2nd ch from hook and in next 6 ch, sc in 2 sc, inc in next sc, sc in next sc, inc in next sc, sc in next 2 sc; working along opposite side of chain, sc in next 6 ch, inc in next ch—24 sc. Remove thread marker and place thread between last st worked and first st on following rnd and carry up as before.

Rnds 4–8: Sc in each sc around.

Rnd 9: Dec over next 2 sc, sc in next 10 sc, dec over next 2 sc, sc in next 8 sc, dec over next 2 sc—21 sc.

Rnd 10: Dec over next 2 sc, sc in next 7 sc, dec over next 2 sc, sc in next sc, dec over next 2 sc, sc in next 7 sc—18 sc. Cut yarn, leaving an 8″ end for sewing. Stuff and sew opening. With front of head facing forward, sew head to neck edge on body.

UPPER LEG SECTION (make four): Ch 8, join with sl st to form ring.

Rnd 1: Ch 1, sc in joining and in each ch around—8 sc; do not join.

Rnd 2: Sc in each sc around. Cut yarn, leaving a 10″ end for sewing. Holding work flat, sew upper edge closed; sew this edge in place on body, referring to photograph for placement.

LOWER LEG (make four): Ch 9.

Row 1: Sc in 2nd ch from hook and in each ch across—8 sc. Ch 1, turn.

Row 2: Sc in each sc across. Cut yarn, leaving a 10″ end for sewing. Fold piece in half and sew starting chain and last row together to form lower leg. Insert a lower leg into opening on upper leg and sew in place.

Cut 4 pieces of pink felt, each ¼″ × 1½″; sew a strip around lower end of each leg to form hoof.

TAIL: Ch 10. Sc in 2nd ch from hook and in each ch across. Cut yarn, leaving an 8″ end for sewing. Sew in place as shown.

FLEECE: Loosely make a chain about 3 yards long and wind into a ball. With sewing thread and leaving small loops of chain free, cover lamb with "fleece" by sewing chain to head, body and upper legs, leaving the first 4 rnds on head and the underside of body free.

Using pattern, cut ears from pink felt and tack in place as shown. Cut out a ¼″ × ¼″ piece of black felt for nose and two small pieces of blue felt for eyes and tack in place.

HEN

SIZE: About 5½″ high.

MATERIALS: Coats & Clark Red Heart® 4-ply crochet yarn, Art. E. 267, one ounce of #286 bronze. Crochet hook size 8/H (5 mm) or size required to obtain gauge. Scraps of red, yellow, tan, black, and white felt. Polyester stuffing.

GAUGE: 4 sts = 1″; 4 rnds = 1″.

HEAD AND BODY: Beg at top of head, ch 3. Join with sl st to form ring.

Rnd 1: Ch 1, 5 sc in ring; do not join rnds but carry a contrasting color thread up between last and first sc to indicate beg of rnds.

Rnd 2: 2 sc in each sc around—10 sc.

Rnd 3–5: 2 sc in next sc—inc made) twice; sc in each sc around—16 sc on rnd 5.

Rnd 6: Sc in each sc around.

Rnd 7: Sc in next 8 sc, (draw up a lp in each of next 2 sc, yo and draw through all 3 lps on hook—dec made) 3 times, sc in next 2 sc—13 sc.

Rnd 8: Cut yarn and fasten off, then sk over next 2 sts, join yarn in next sc, ch 8 for back extension, sc in 2nd ch from hook, sc in next 6 ch; working over sts on last rnd, inc in next sc, sc in next 10 sc, 2 sc in next sc; working along opposite side of chain, sc in next 6 ch, inc in next ch—29 sc. Place thread marker between last st worked and next st as before.

Rnd 9–11: Sc in each sc around.

Rnd 12: Sc in next 6 sc, inc in next sc, sc in next 16 sc, inc in next sc, sc in next 5 sc—31 sc.

Rnd 13–15: Sc in each sc around.

Rnd 16: Sc in next 14 sc, (dec over next 2 sc) twice; sc in next 13 sc—29 sc. Remove thread marker. Shape underside of body as follows: Stuffing body as work progresses, * sc in next sc, dec over next 2 sc. Repeat from * around until opening is 1″ in diameter. Leaving a 10″ length for sewing, cut yarn; draw yarn end through remaining sts; pull sts together and secure.

WING (make two): Ch 4.

Row 1: Sc in 2nd ch from hook and in next 2 ch—3 sc. Ch 1, turn.

Row 2: Sc in each sc across. Ch 7, turn. Form wing feathers as follows:

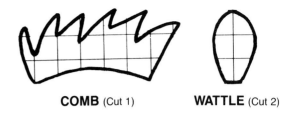

PATTERNS FOR HEN
Each square represents ¼″

COMB (Cut 1)   **WATTLE** (Cut 2)

FOOT (Cut 2)   **BEAK** (Cut 1)

Row 3: Sl st in 2nd ch from hook and in next 5 ch, sl st in first sc, ch 5, sl st in 2nd ch from hook and in next 3 ch, sl st in next sc, ch 3, sl st in 2nd ch from hook and in next ch, sl st in last sc. Fasten off. Cut ⅛″-wide strips of tan felt and sew along the chain sections on wing feathers. Sew wings to body as shown.

TAIL: Ch 4.

Row 1: Sc in 2nd ch from hook and in next 2 ch—3 sc. Ch 4, turn.

Row 2: Sl st in 2nd ch from hook and in next 2 ch, sl st in first sc, ch 3, sl st in 2nd ch from hook and in next ch, sl st in next sc, ch 2, sl st in 2nd ch from hook and in last sc. Fasten off. Sew tail to body as shown.

LEG AND FOOT (make two): Cut a piece of yellow felt ½″ × 1″ for leg. Starting with the ½″ edge, roll piece up tightly to make leg; sew ½″ edge in place to keep from unrolling. Using pattern, cut foot from yellow felt and sew to end of leg. Sew legs in place.

EYE (make two): Cut a round piece of white felt ⅜″ in diameter and a ¼″ round piece of black felt. Glue black felt on top of white felt and glue in place.

BEAK: From yellow felt cut beak, following pattern. Sew edges A and B together and sew edge C in place on head as shown.

Using patterns, cut comb and wattle from red felt and tack in place as shown.

Scotties, Scotties Everywhere

Coordinate your child's room with these loveable Scottie-motif accessories that include a pillow toy, loop stitch rug, wall hanging and afghan. The wall hanging comes with pockets—the perfect places to store a child's treasured possessions.

SCOTTIE RUG

SIZE: 18″ × 27″.

MATERIALS: Worsted weight yarn, three 100-gram (3.5-oz.) skeins camel (A), one skein each black (B) and red (C). Crochet hook size 6/G (4.25 mm) or size required to obtain gauge. Rug canvas, 18″ × 27″.

GAUGE: 16 sts = 4″; 17 rows = 4″.

Note: When working from chart, do not carry colors across wrong side of work; use separate balls as required, picking up next color from under dropped color to prevent holes in work. Cut and join colors as necessary.

LOOP STITCH PAT: Row 1 (right side): Sc in 2nd ch from hook and in each ch across. Ch 1, turn.

Row 2: * Insert hook in next st, wind yarn back around right index finger to make a loop 1″ long, draw yarn coming from left index finger through st, drop loop from finger, yo and through 2 lps on hook—loop st made—repeat from * across. Ch 1, turn.

Row 3: Sc in each st across. Ch 1, turn. Repeat rows 2 and 3 for pat.

RUG: With A, ch 21. Work row 1 of loop st pat—20 sc. See row 1 of chart. Ch 4 to inc 3 sts as shown on chart.

Row 2: Loop st in 2nd ch from hook and in next 2 ch, work row 2 of loop st pat across—23 sts. Ch 4 to inc 3 sts as shown on chart.

Row 3: Sc in 2nd ch from hook and in next 2 ch, work row 3 of loop st pat across—26 sts. Continue in this manner, following chart for incs until row 24 is completed. Ch 2, turn.

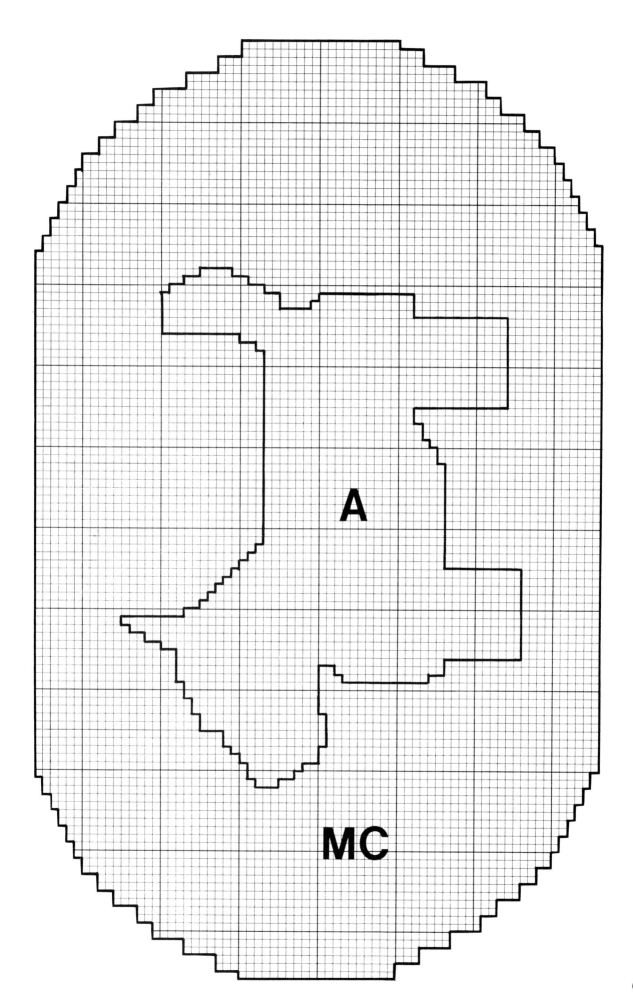

A

MC

Row 25: Sc in 2nd ch from hook, sc in next 39 sts; join B and work 3 sc; with another skein of A, sc to end. Ch 2, turn.

Row 26: Loop st in 2nd ch from hook and in next 26 sts; with A, work 6 loop sts; with A, loop st to end. Ch 2, turn.

Row 27: Sc in 2nd ch from hook and in next 37 sts; with B, work 7 sc; with A, sc to end. Ch 1, turn. Work even in pat from chart until row 90 is completed. Work decs as shown on chart: at beg of row, sl st across number of sts to be decreased; at end of row, leave sts unworked. Work to end of chart; end off.

COLLAR: With C, ch 40. Work 3 rows of 39 sc. End off. Fold collar in half crosswise and sew to scottie across neck.

FACING: From right side of rug, with A, work a 2″ border of sc around rug, decreasing at curved ends to keep work flat against wrong side of rug. End off, leaving a long end for sewing. Cut rug canvas to oval shape of rug and slip under facing. Sew facing to canvas.

SCOTTIE PILLOW

SIZE: 17″ × 13″.

MATERIALS: Worsted weight yarn, three 100-gram (3.5-oz.) skeins black (A), one ball red (B). Crochet hook size 6/G (4.25 mm) or size required to obtain gauge. One bag polyester stuffing. Two ⅝″ black buttons. Scrap of red felt. One 1⅜″ I.D. tag.

GAUGE: 16 sts = 4″; 17 rows = 4″ (loop st pat).

LOOP ST: * Insert hook in next st, wind yarn back around right index finger to make a loop 1″ long, draw yarn coming from left index finger through st, drop loop from finger, yo and through 2 lps on hook—loop st made; repeat from * across.

PILLOW: LEFT SIDE: With A, ch 51.

Row 1 (right side): Sc in 2nd ch from hook and in each ch across—50 sc. Ch 1, turn.

Row 2: Loop st in each sc. Ch 1, turn.

Row 3: Sc in each st. Ch 1, turn.

Rows 4–12: Repeat rows 2 and 3, 4 times, then row 2 once more.

Row 13: Sc to last st, sk last st—49 sts. Ch 1, turn.

Row 14: Sk first st, loop st to end—48 sts.

Row 15: Repeat row 13—47 sts.

Row 16: Repeat row 2.

Row 17: Repeat row 13—46 sts.

Row 18: Repeat row 14—45 sts.

Row 19: Repeat row 3.

Chin: Row 20: Ch 13; sc in 2nd ch from hook, loop st in next 11 ch, loop st to last st, sk last sc—56 sts. Ch 1, turn.

Row 21: Sk first st, sc in each st across—55 sts. Ch 2, turn.

Row 22: Sc in 2nd ch from hook, loop st in each st across—56 sts. Ch 1, turn.

Row 23: Repeat row 3. Ch 2, turn.

Row 24: Repeat row 22—57 sts. Ch 3, turn.

Row 25: Sc in 2nd ch from hook and in next ch, sc in each st across—59 sts. Ch 2, turn.

Row 26: Repeat row 22—60 sts. Ch 2, turn.

Tail: Row 27: Sc in 2nd ch from hook and in next 7 sts—8 sts. Ch 1, turn.

Row 28: Sk first st, loop st in each st—7 sts. Ch 2, turn.

Row 29: Repeat row 27—8 sts. Ch 1, turn.

Row 30: Repeat row 28—7 sts. Ch 1, turn.

Rows 31 and 33: Repeat row 3.

Rows 32, 34, 36 and 38: Repeat row 2.

Rows 35 and 37: Sk first st, sc in each st across—5 sts. Ch 1, turn.

Row 39: Repeat row 35—4 sts. End off.

Head: Row 40: From right side, sk 24 sts on last long row; join A in next st, sc in same st and in each st to end—29 sc. Ch 2, turn.

Row 41: Sc in 2nd ch from hook, loop st to last st, sk last st. Ch 1, turn.

Row 42: Sk first st, sc in each st across—28 sc. Ch 1, turn.

Row 43: Sk first st, loop st to last st, sk last st—26 sts. Ch 1, turn.

Row 44: Sk first st, sc to last 3 sts, sk last 3 sts—22 sc. Ch 1, turn.

Row 45: Sk first st, loop st to last st, sk last st—20 sts. Ch 1, turn.

Row 46: Sk first st, sc to last st, sk last st—18 sc.

Row 47: Sk first 2 sts, loop st to last st, sk last st—15 sts.

Row 48: Repeat row 46—13 sc. Ch 1, turn.

Row 49: Sk first st, loop st in each st—12 sts. Ch 1, turn.

Row 50: Sc to last st, sk last st—11 sts. Ch 1, turn.

Row 51: Repeat row 45—9 sts. End off.

Front Leg: Row 52: From right side with A, sc in each of first 34 sts on starting ch. Ch 2, turn.

Row 53: Sk first 2 sts, loop st to last st, sk last st—31 sts.

Row 54: Sk first st, sc to last st, sk last st—29 sts. Ch 2, turn.

Row 55: Repeat row 53—26 sts.

Row 56: Sk first 2 sts, sc in next 11 sts. Work even in pat on 11 sts for 9 rows. End off.

Back Leg: Row 66: From right side, sk 2 sts on starting ch after front leg, work sc in next 12 sts. Ch 1, turn.

Row 67: Sk first st, loop st in each st across—11 sts. Ch 1, turn.

Rows 68–77: Repeat rows 3 and 2, 5 times. End off.

RIGHT SIDE: With A, ch 12. End off; set ch aside. Work right side as for left side through row 12.

Row 13: Sk first st, sc in each st across—49 sts. Ch 1, turn.

Row 14: Loop st to last st, sk last st—48 sts. Ch 1, turn.

Row 15: Repeat row 13—47 sts.

Row 16: Repeat row 2.

Row 17: Repeat row 13—46 sts.

Row 18: Repeat row 14—45 sts.

Row 19: Repeat row 3.

Chin: Row 20: Sk first st, loop st in each st across, loop st in each ch of ch-12 that was set aside—56 sts. Ch 1, turn.

Row 21: Sc to last st, sk last st—55 sc. Ch 1, turn.

Row 22: Repeat row 2. Ch 2, turn.

Row 23: Sc in 2nd ch from hook and in each st across—56 sc. Ch 1, turn.

Row 24: Repeat row 2. Ch 2, turn.

Row 25: Repeat row 23—57 sts. Ch 3, turn.

Row 26: Sc in 2nd ch from hook, loop st in next ch and in each st across—57 sts. Ch 2, turn.

Head: Row 27: Sc in 2nd ch from hook and in next 28 sts—29 sts. Ch 1, turn.

Row 28: Sk first st, loop st in each st across—28 sts. Ch 1, turn.

Row 29: Sc to last st, sk last st—27 sts. Ch 1, turn.

Row 30: Sk first st, loop st to last st, sk last st—25 sts.

Row 31: Sl st across 3 sts, sc in next st and each st to last st, sk last st—21 sts. Ch 1, turn.

Row 32: Repeat row 30—19 sts. Ch 1, turn.

Row 33: Sk first st, sc to last st, sk last st—17 sts. Ch 1, turn.

Row 34: Sk first st, loop st to last 2 sts, sk last 2 sts—14 sts. Ch 1, turn.

Row 35: Repeat row 33—12 sts. Ch 1, turn.

Row 36: Loop st to last st, sk last st—11 sts. Ch 1, turn.

Row 37: Sk first st, sc in each st across—10 sc.

Row 38: Repeat row 30—8 sts. End off.

Tail: Row 39: From right side, sk 24 sts on last long row, sc in each of last 7 sts. Ch 2, turn.

Row 40: Sc in 2nd ch from hook, loop st to last st, sk last st—7 sts.

Rows 41, 43 and 45: Repeat row 3. Ch 2, turn.

Row 42: Repeat row 40.

Rows 44, 46, 48 and 50: Repeat row 2.

Row 47: Sc to last st, sk last st—6 sts.

Row 49: Repeat row 47—5 sts.

Row 51: Repeat row 47—4 sts. End off.

Back Leg: Row 52: From right side with A, sk 2 sts on opposite side of starting ch, sc in each of next 12 sts. Ch 1, turn.

Row 53: Loop st to last st, sk last st—11 sts.

Rows 54–63: Repeat rows 2 and 3, 5 times. End off.

Front Leg: Row 64: Sk 2 sts on starting ch after back leg, sc in each st to end—34 sts. Ch 1, turn.

Row 65: Sk first st, loop st to last 2 sts, sk last 2 sts—31 sts. Ch 1, turn.

Row 66: Sk first st, sc to last st, sk last st—29 sts. Ch 1, turn.

Row 67: Repeat row 65—26 sts. End off. Turn.

Row 68: Sk 13 sts, sc in next st and in each st to last sts, sk last 2 sts—11 sts. Ch 1, turn.

Row 69: Repeat row 3.

Rows 70–77: Repeat rows 2 and 3, 4 times. End off.

GUSSET: With A, ch 8. Sc in 2nd ch from hook and in each ch across—7 sts. Work rows 2 and 3 on 7 sts until piece is about 75″ long, sewing one edge to edge of one scottie piece as you go along. Sew remaining scottie piece to gusset, leaving 5″ opening for stuffing. Stuff pillow lightly. Sew opening closed.

EARS: With A, ch 15. Sc in 2nd ch from hook and in each ch—14 sc. Ch 1, turn.

Next Row: Sk first st, sc in each sc across—13 sc. Ch 1, turn. Repeat last row until 1 st remains. Work 1 row sc around ear. End off. Sew ears in curved shape to top of head.

COLLAR: With B, ch 65. Work 2 rows sc. End off. Place collar around neck; sew ends together.

FINISHING: Attach I.D. tag to collar. Sew on button eyes. Cut 1″-long tongue from red felt; sew in place.

SCOTTIE WALL HANGING

SIZE: 16″ × 23″.

MATERIALS: Worsted weight yarn, two 100-gram (3.5-oz.) skeins red (A), one skein each camel (B) and black (C), Crochet hooks sizes 3/D (3.25 mm), 6/G (4.25 mm) and 8/H (5 mm) or size required to obtain gauge. Three 1½″ bone rings.

GAUGE: 7 sts = 2″; 6 rows = 2″ (hdc, with largest hook).

WALL HANGING: MAIN SECTION: With A and largest hook, ch 53.

Row 1 (right side): Hdc in 3rd ch from hook and in each ch across—51 hdc. Ch 2, turn.

Row 2: Hdc in each hdc across. Ch 2, turn.

Rows 3–63: Repeat row 2. End off.

Border: Rnd 1: From right side, with C and largest hook, work 1 rnd sc evenly around, working 3 sc in each corner. Join with sl st in first sc. End off.

Rnd 2: From right side, with B and largest hook, join yarn in any st, ch 1 * draw up a lp in st just worked, yo, draw up a lp in same st, sk 1 st, yo, draw up a lp in next st, yo, draw up a lp in same st, yo and through all 8 lps on hook, ch 1, repeat from * around. Join with sl st in top of first cluster. End off.

SMALL POCKET: With B and largest hook, ch 33.

Row 1 (wrong side): Hdc in 3rd ch from hook and in each ch across—31 hdc. Ch 2, turn.

Rows 2–12: Hdc in each hdc across. Ch 2, turn. At end of last row, ch 1, sc down side of pocket, across bottom edge and up other side of pocket, working 3 sc in each corner. End off. With C, work 1 rnd sc around all 4 sides of pocket. Join with sl st in first sc. End off.

MEDIUM POCKET: With B and largest hook, ch 39. Work as for small pocket on 37 sts for 14 rows. Finish as for small pocket.

LARGE POCKET: With B and largest hook, ch 45. Work as for small pocket on 43 sts for 16 rows. Finish as for small pocket.

SCOTTIE (make two with smallest hook, two with medium-size hook, and two with largest hook): With C, ch 17.

Row 1: Sc in 2nd ch from hook and in each ch across—16 sc. Ch 1, turn.

Rows 2–5: Sc in each sc. Ch 1, turn.

Row 6: Sk first sc, sc in each of 15 sc. Ch 6 for chin, turn.

Row 7: Sc in 2nd ch from hook and in next 4 ch, sc in 14 sc—19 sc. Ch 2, turn.

Tail: Row 8: Sc in 2nd ch from hook and in next 2 sc. Ch 1, turn.

Row 9: Sk first sc, sc in next 2 sc. Ch 1, turn.

Row 10: Sc in 2 sc. Ch 1, turn.

Row 11: Sk first sc, sc in next sc. Ch 1, turn.

Row 12: Sc in sc. End off.

Head: Row 13: Make lp on hook, sc in first sc of last long row and in next 9 sc. Ch 1, turn.

Row 14: Sk first sc, sc in 9 sc. Ch 1, turn.

Row 15: Sk first sc, sc in 8 sc. Ch 1, turn.

Row 16: Sk first sc, sc in 7 sc. Ch 1, turn.

Row 17: Sk first sc, sc in 6 sc. Ch 4 for ear, turn.

Row 18: Sc in 2nd ch from hook, hdc in next 2 ch, sk 2 sc, sc in next sc. End off.

Back Leg: Working on opposite side of starting ch, sk first ch at tail end, sc in next 5 sts. Ch 1, turn.

Next Row: Sk first sc, sc in 4 sc. Ch 1, turn. Work 2 more rows of 4 sc. End off.

Front Leg: Sk 2 ch from end of first row of back leg, join yarn in next ch, ch 1, sc in next 7 sts. Ch 1, turn.

Next Row: Sc in 3 sc. Ch 1, turn. Work 2 more rows of 3 sc. End off.

Collar: With C, ch 14. End off. Tie around neck. Tack in place.

FINISHING: Sew scotties on pockets as pictured. Center and space pockets evenly on main section. Sew to main section along sides and bottom of pockets.

Hanging Rings: With medium-size hook and B, sc closely around ring. Join with sl st in first sc. End off, leaving a long end for sewing. Sew rings to top edge of wall hanging, one at each corner, one at center.

SCOTTIE AFGHAN

SIZE: 40″ × 50″.

MATERIALS: Worsted weight yarn, eight 100-gram (3.5-oz.) skeins camel (A), two skeins black (B), 1 skein red (C). Crochet hook size 8/H (5 mm) or size needed to obtain gauge. Black sewing thread.

GAUGE: 7 sts = 2″; 6 rows = 2″ (hdc). Each square is 9½″ × 9½″.

AFGHAN: SQUARE (make twenty): With A, ch 31.

Row 1 (wrong side): Hdc in 3rd ch from hook and in each ch across—29 hdc. Ch 2, turn.

Row 2: Hdc in first st and in each st across. Ch 2, turn.

Rows 3–24: Repeat row 2. At end of last row, turn.

Border: Rnd 1 (wrong side): Sl st in first st, ch 3 (counts as hdc, ch 1), * sk 1 st, yo hook, pull up a lp in next st, yo and through 2 lps, (yo hook, pull up a lp in same st, yo and through 2 lps) 3 times, yo and through all 5 lps on hook—cluster made; (ch 1, sk 1 st, hdc in next st, ch 1, sk 1 st, cluster in next st) 6 times, ch 1, sk 1 st, hdc in last st, ch 2, cluster in end of last row, ch 2, hdc in next row, (ch 1, cluster in next row, ch 1, sk 1 row, hdc in next row) 3 times, ch 1, cluster between next 2 rows, ch 1, sk 1 row, (hdc in next row, ch 1, sk 1 row, cluster in next row, ch 1) 3 times, hdc in next row, ch 2, cluster in end of last row, ch 2, * hdc in first st, ch 1, repeat from first * to 2nd * once, sl st in 2nd ch of ch-3. Ch 1, turn.

Rnd 2: Sc in each st and ch around, working 3 sc in each corner cluster. End off.

SCOTTIE (make ten): With B, ch 17.

Row 1: Sc in 2nd ch from hook and in each ch across—16 sc. Ch 1, turn.

Rows 2–5: Sc in each sc. Ch 1, turn.

Row 6: Sk first sc, sc in each of 15 sc. Ch 6 for chin, turn.

Row 7: Sc in 2nd ch from hook and in next 4 ch, sc in 14 sc—19 sc. Ch 2, turn.

Tail: Row 8: Sc in 2nd ch from hook and in next 2 sc. Ch 1, turn.

Row 9: Sk first sc, sc in next 2 sc. Ch 1, turn.

Row 10: Sc in 2 sc. Ch 1, turn.

Row 11: Sk first sc, sc in next sc. Ch 1, turn.

Row 12: Sc in sc. End off.

Head: Row 13: Make lp on hook, sc in first sc of last long row and in next 9 sc. Ch 1, turn.

Row 14: Sk first sc, sc in 9 sc. Ch 1, turn.

Row 15: Sk first sc, sc in 8 sc. Ch 1, turn.

Row 16: Sk first sc, sc in 7 sc. Ch 1, turn.

Row 17: Sk first sc, sc in 6 sc. Ch 4 for ear, turn.

Row 18: Sc in 2nd ch from hook, hdc in next 2 ch, sk 2 sc, sc in next sc. End off.

Back Leg: Working on opposite side of starting ch, sk first ch at tail end, sc in next 5 sts. Ch 1, turn.

Next Row: Sk first sc, sc in 4 sc. Ch 1, turn. Work 2 more rows of 4 sc. End off.

Front Leg: Sk 2 ch from end of first row of back leg, join yarn in next ch, ch 1, sc in next 7 sts. Ch 1, turn.

Next Row: Sc in 3 sc. Ch 1, turn. Work 2 more rows of 3 sc. End off.

Collar: With C, ch 14. End off. Tie around neck. Tack in place.

FINISHING: Sew Scottie to center of square, facing right or left as indicated by arrows on chart. Sew squares tog on wrong side with A, sewing through back lps of sc (lps nearest you).

Border: Rnd 1: From right side, join B in any sc, ch 1, * draw up a lp in st just worked, yo, draw up a lp in same st, sk 1 st, yo, draw up a lp in next st, yo, draw up a lp in same st, yo and through all 8 lps on hook, ch 1, repeat from * around, keeping work flat; join with a sl st in top of first cluster. End off.

Rnd 2: From right side, join C in any sp between clusters, ch 1, * draw up a lp in last sp worked, yo, draw up a lp in same sp, yo, draw up a lp in next sp between clusters, yo, draw up a lp in same sp, yo and through all 8 lps on hook, ch 1; repeat from * around. Join with sl st in top of first cluster. End off.

Braided Chain Trimming: Join C with sc in first sc of first square at left on lower edge of afghan where first and 2nd squares are joined. Ch 3, sk 3 sc on edge of 2nd square, sc in next sc, drop lp from hook; join B with sc in first sc of 2nd square at lower edge, ch 3, sk 2 sc on edge of first square, sc in next sc, ch 3, sk 2 sc on edge of 2nd square, sc in next sc, drop lp from hook. * Pick up C lp, ch 3, sk 2 sc on first square, sc in next sc, ch 3, sk 2 sc on 2nd square, sc in next sc, drop lp from hook; pick up B lp, ch 3, sk 2 sc on first square, sc in next sc, ch 3, sk 2 sc on 2nd square, sc in next sc, drop lp from hook; repeat from * to top of afghan. End off. Work same trimming over other two vertical seams. Work same trimming over horizontal seams.

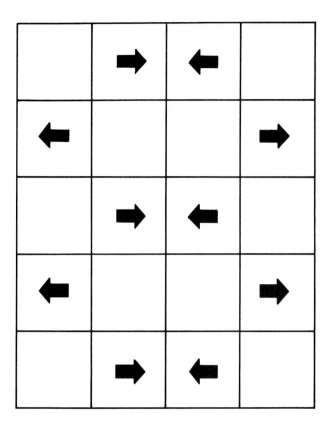

Arrows indicate directions motifs face

Games Children Play

Here is a unique crocheted game board for checkers or chess. It's portable and can be rolled up for easy storage. It makes a great carry-along on family vacations, and the playing pieces will never get lost when kept in their own labeled pouch.

SIZE: 13" square.

MATERIALS: Coats & Clark Red Heart® 100% cotton yarn, three skeins flame #902 (A), two skeins black #12 (B). Afghan hook size 5/F (3.75 mm). Crochet hook size 4/E (3.5 mm) or size required to obtain gauge. J. & P. Coats Deluxe Six Strand Floss, one skein black. Embroidery needle. Black felt, 13" square. Black sewing thread.

GAUGE: 9 sts = 2"; 3 rows = 1".

BOARD: With A and afghan hook, ch 48.

Row 1: Keeping all lps on hook, pull up a lp in 2nd ch from hook and in each of next 4 ch, drop A to wrong side; * with B, pull up a lp in each of next 6 ch, drop B to wrong side; with A, pull up a lp in each of next 6 ch, drop A to wrong side; repeat from * across, end with B, pull up a lp in each of last 6 ch—48 lps on hook.

To Work Lps Off: Yo hook, pull through first lp, (yo hook, pull through next 2 lps) 5 times, drop B; * pick up A from under dropped strand; with A, (yo hook, pull through next 2 lps) 6 times, drop A; pick up B from under dropped strand; with B, (yo hook, pull through next 2 lps) 6 times, drop B; repeat from * across until 1 A lp remains. Lp that remains on hook always counts as first st of next row.

Rows 2–4: Keeping all lps on hook, sk first vertical bar, pull up a lp under next vertical bar and under each vertical bar across, working in same colors as previous row. Work lps off in same colors as before.

Rows 5–8: Work in opposite colors, B block over A block, A block over B block.

Continue as established for 32 rows from beg, changing blocks of color every 4 rows. With matching colors, sl st in each vertical bar across. End off.

Border: Rnd 1: Join A with sc in corner st, sc around board, working 5 sc in each block, sc, ch 1, sc in each of next 3 corners. At end of rnd, work 2 sc in corner st. Ch 1, turn.

Rnds 2–4: Sc in each sc around, sc, ch 1, sc in each of next 3 corner ch—1 sps, 2 sc in last sc. Ch 1, turn. Cut yarn, leaving an end for sewing. Sew corner seam.

FINISHING: Sew felt square to wrong side of board.

BAG (make two pieces): Beg at top with A and crochet hook, ch 16.

Row 1: Sc in 2nd ch from hook and in each ch—15 sc. Ch 1, turn.

Rows 2–21: Sc in each sc. Ch 1, turn each row.

Row 22: Sc across to last 2 sts, pull up a lp in each of last 2 sts, yo and through 3 lps on hook—1 dec made. Repeat row 22 until 9 sc remain. End off.

FINISHING: With embroidery floss, embroider CHESS in chain st vertically on one piece, following chart (see Embroidery Stitch Details, page 78). Sew pieces together to form bag. Using double strand of floss, crochet a 24" chain. Weave through row 4 of bag to tie at side. Make a knot at each end of tie.

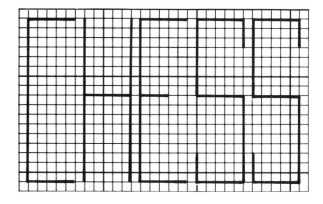

CROCHET BASICS

Here are general instructions for making the crochet projects in this book. Crochet hooks come in various sizes—the size you use will depend on the yarns, patterns, and projects that you make.

It will be helpful to read the instructions here before beginning your projects.

CROCHET ABBREVIATIONS

ch—chain stitch	**sc**—single crochet
st—stitch	**sl st**—slip stitch
sts—stitches	**dc**—double crochet
lp—loop	**hdc**—half double crochet
inc—increase	**tr**—treble or triple crochet
dec—decrease	**dtr**—double treble crochet
rnd—round	**tr tr**—treble treble crochet
beg—beginning	**bl**—block
sk—skip	**sp**—space
p—picot	**cl**—cluster
tog—together	**pat**—pattern
lp—loop	**yo**—yarn over hook

HOW TO FOLLOW DIRECTIONS

An asterisk (*) is often used in crochet directions to indicate repetition. For example, when directions read, "* 2 dc in next st, 1 dc in next st, repeat from * four times," this means to work directions after first * four times more. Work five times in all.

When parentheses ( ) are used to show repetition, work directions within the parentheses as many times as specified. For example, "(dc, ch 1) three times" means to do what is within ( ) three times altogether.

"Work even" in directions means to work in the same pattern stitch on the same number of stitches, without increasing or decreasing.

CHAIN STITCH (ch)

To make first loop on hook, grasp yarn about 2 inches from end between left thumb and index finger. With right hand, lap long strand over short end, forming a loop. Hold loop in place with left thumb and index finger.

Figure 1: Grasp hook in right hand, insert hook through loop, catch strand with hook and draw it

Fig. 1

through loop. Pull end and long strand in opposite directions to close loop around hook.

Drawing the yarn through the loop on the hook makes this chain stitch. Repeat step until you have as many chains as you need. One loop always remains on hook. Practice making all chains uniform.

Fig. 2

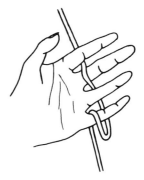

Figure 2: Weave yarn through left hand.

SINGLE CROCHET (sc)

Fig. 1

Figure 1: Insert hook in second chain from hook. Yarn over hook.

Fig. 2

Figure 2: Draw yarn through chain—2 loops on hook.

Fig. 3

Figure 3: Yarn over hook. Draw yarn through 2 loops on hook. One single crochet has been made.

Fig. 4

Figure 4: Work a single crochet in each chain stitch. At end of row, chain 1 and turn work around.

Fig. 5

Figure 5: Insert hook under both top loops of stitch below, yarn over hook and draw through stitch. Yarn over and through 2 loops on hook. Work a single crochet in same way in each stitch across row.

Fig. 6

Figure 6: To make a ridge stitch or slipper stitch, work rows of single crochet by inserting hook in back loop only of each single crochet.

HOW TO INCREASE 1 SINGLE CROCHET (inc)

Work 2 stitches in 1 stitch.

HOW TO DECREASE 1 SINGLE CROCHET (dec)

Pull up a loop in 1 stitch, pull up a loop in next stitch (3 loops on hook), yarn over hook, draw through all 3 loops at once.

SLIP STITCH (sl st)

Insert hook in work. Yarn over hook and draw through both the stitch and the loop on hook. Slip stitch makes a firm finishing edge. A single slip stitch is used for joining a chain to form a ring.

HALF-DOUBLE CROCHET (hdc)

Fig. 1

Figure 1: Yarn over hook. Insert hook in third chain from hook.

Figure 2: Yarn over hook, draw through chain. Yarn over hook again.

Figure 3: Draw through all 3 loops on hook. One half-double crochet has been made.

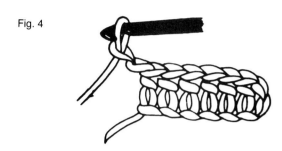

Figure 4: Work a half-double crochet in each chain across. At end of row, chain 2 and turn work.

DOUBLE CROCHET (dc)

Figure 1: Yarn over hook. Insert hook in fourth chain from hook.

Figure 2: Yarn over hook. Draw through chain. There are 3 loops on hook.

Figure 3: Yarn over hook. Draw through 2 loops on hook. There are 2 loops on hook. Yarn over hook.

Figure 4: Draw yarn through remaining 2 loops on hook. One double crochet has been made. When you have worked a double crochet in each chain across, chain 3 and turn work. In most directions, the turning chain-3 counts as first double crochet of next row. In working the second row, skip the first stitch and work a double crochet in the 2 top loops of each double crochet across. The last double crochet of each row is worked in the top chain of the chain-3 turning chain.

TREBLE OR TRIPLE CROCHET (tr)

With 1 loop on hook, put yarn over hook twice, insert in fifth chain from hook, pull loop through. Yarn over and draw through 2 loops at a time three times. At end of a row, chain 4 and turn. Chain-4 counts as first treble of next row.

DOUBLE TREBLE (dtr)

Put yarn over hook three times and work off 2 loops at a time as for treble.

TREBLE TREBLE (tr tr)

Put yarn over hook four times and work off 2 loops at a time as for treble.

PLAIN AFGHAN STITCH

Work with afghan hook. Make a chain desired length.

Figure 1: Row 1: Keeping all loops on hook, skip first chain from hook (loop on hook is first stitch), pull up a loop in each chain across.

Figure 2: To Work Loops Off: Yarn over hook, pull through first loop, * yarn over hook, pull

through next 2 loops, repeat from * across until 1 loop remains. Loop that remains on hook always counts as first stitch of next row.

Fig. 3

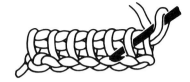

Figure 3: Row 2: Keeping all loops on hook, skip first vertical bar (loop on hook is first stitch), pull up a loop under next vertical bar and under each vertical bar across. Work loops off as before. Repeat row 2 for plain afghan stitch.

Edge Stitch: Made at end of rows only to make a firm edge. Work as follows: Insert hook under last vertical bar and in loop at back of bar, pull up 1 loop.

HALF CROSS-STITCH ON AFGHAN STITCH

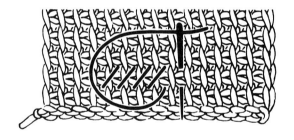

CROSS-STITCH ON AFGHAN STITCH

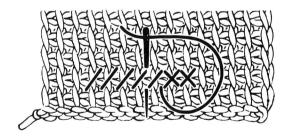

HOW TO TURN YOUR WORK

In crochet a certain number of chain stitches are needed at the end of each row to bring work into position for the next row. Then the work is turned so reverse side is facing the crocheter. Follow the stitch table below for the number of chain stitches to make a turn.

Single crochet (sc)	Ch 1 to turn
Half-double crochet (half dc or hdc)	Ch 2 to turn
Double crochet (dc)	Ch 3 to turn
Treble crochet (tr)	Ch 4 to turn
Double treble crochet (dtr)	Ch 5 to turn
Treble treble crochet (tr tr)	Ch 6 to turn

EMBROIDERY STITCH DETAILS

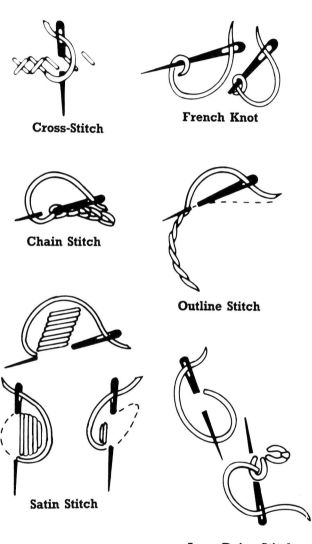

Cross-Stitch

French Knot

Chain Stitch

Outline Stitch

Satin Stitch

Lazy Daisy Stitch

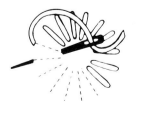

Straight Stitch

INDEX

All of us at Meredith® Press are dedicated to offering you, our customer, the best books we can create. We are particularly concerned that all of the instructions for making the projects are clear and accurate. We welcome your comments and would like to hear any suggestions you may have. Please address your correspondence to Customer Service Department, Meredith® Press, Meredith Corporation, 150 East 52nd Street, New York, NY 10022.